RANDALL JARRELL
and the
Lost World of Childhood

Randall Jarrell in 1926, with his father, Owen Jarrell,
and his paternal grandmother and great-grandmother.
(Courtesy of Mary Jarrell)

RANDALL JARRELL
and the
Lost World of Childhood

Richard Flynn

The University of Georgia Press

Athens and London

© 1990 by the University of Georgia Press
Athens, Georgia 30602

Copyright credits for quotations reprinted here
appear on pages xii–xiii of this book.

All rights reserved
Set in Fairfield Medium and Deepdene
Typeset by Tseng Information Systems, Inc.
Printed and bound by Thomson-Shore, Inc.
The paper in this book meets the guidelines for
permanence and durability of the Committee on
Production Guidelines for Book Longevity of the
Council on Library Resources.

Printed in the United States of America

94 93 92 91 90   5 4 3 2 1

Library of Congress Cataloging in Publication Data

Flynn, Richard.
Randall Jarrell and the lost world of childhood / Richard Flynn.
p. cm.
Includes bibliographical references.
ISBN 0-8203-1243-6 (alk. paper)
1. Jarrell, Randall, 1914–1965—Criticism and interpretation.
2. Children in literature.   3. Family in literature.   4. Youth in
literature.   I. Title.
PS3519.A86Z65   1990
811'.52—dc20   90-30033
                                                    CIP

British Library Cataloging in Publication Data available

Chapter 6 appeared in different form in *Children's Literature*,
vol. 16, edited by Francelia Butler, Margaret R. Higonnet,
and Barbara Rosen (Yale University Press, 1988).

For my son, Richard Nicholas Flynn
and
In memory of my mother,
Joanne Resseguie Flynn
(1930–1990)

Contents

Preface

In his well-known self interview, James Dickey's "B" voice joins a number of critics who fault Randall Jarrell's work for its apparent sentimentality ("Randall Jarrell" 33–48). Perhaps the most insightful defense to this perennial criticism is the one given by Jarrell himself in "Poets, Critics, and Readers" (1959):

> Ordinary human feeling, the most natural tenderness, will seem to many critics and readers rank sentimentality, just as a kind of nauseated brutality (in which the writer's main response to the world is simply to vomit) will seem to many critics and readers the inescapable truth. We live in a time in which Hofmannsthal's "Good taste is the ability continuously to counteract exaggeration" will seem to many readers as false as it seems tame. "Each epoch has its own sentimentality," Hofmannsthal goes on, "its specific way of overemphasizing strata of emotion. The sentimentality of the present is egoistic and unloving; it exaggerates not the feeling of love but that of the self." (*Sad Heart* 98)

As Dickey's "A" persona admits, ordinary human feeling, natural tenderness, and the deflation of exaggeration are at the heart of Randall Jarrell's work, and nowhere are these qualities more powerfully evoked than in Jarrell's image of the role of the child in the twentieth century:

> [Jarrell's poems] show in front of you a child's slow, horrified, magnificently un-understanding and growing loss of innocence in which we all share and can't help. . . . The poems are one long look, through this ex-

pression, into a child's face, as the Things of modern life happen around
it, happen to it. . . . Now *that* is our time. It is humanity in the twentieth
century. (47–48)

Among twentieth-century poets, Jarrell best chronicles the paradox
implicit in this statement. As Neil Postman and others argue, the very
social forces which made the invention of childhood necessary—the
rise of the middle class, industrialization, modern warfare, and a host
of other factors that have led modern Americans increasingly to think
of the family as what Christopher Lasch calls "a haven in a heartless
world"—are the same forces which conspire to fragment the family
and relegate the child to a position in which its life is devalued. The
rise of the idea of childhood as we know it is largely a legacy of Romanticism, and as Jarrell points out in "The End of the Line," modernism
carried Romantic principles to their absurd and fragmented conclusion. As a poet writing in the shadow of the great modernists, Jarrell
sought, tentatively at first, his own poetic voice as well as his own
poetic subjects. His insight into the twentieth century's loss of the
idea of childhood, of what many perceive as its tragic devaluation of
both the life of the actual child and that of the residual child within
the adult, represents his greatest contribution to our poetry and to our
intellectual and emotional life. In an early poem, Jarrell has the world
personified say, "Child, your life is cheaper than a wrench." Jarrell's
lifelong enterprise was to counteract this judgment and to restore to us
some measure of our humanity.

"The ways we miss our lives are life," Jarrell observes in "A Girl in a
Library"; it seems to me pertinent to add that we miss, sometimes, the
"real" Randall Jarrell, because of both his enthusiasms and his reti-
cence. Although I have drawn on Jarrell's often difficult, but usually
rewarding, life in order to illuminate the work, the work takes prece-
dence. In our age we see daily the flickering images from our television
screens resolve into a "child's set face"; it is important that we attend
to Jarrell's lost worlds, as well as to our own, in order to live somewhat
hopefully in a world that seems increasingly hopeless.

Acknowledgments

I have been assisted by many people in my attempt to present the "real" Randall Jarrell. First and foremost, I am thankful to Mary Jarrell who, in our many conversations, has been generous, forthright, and enthusiastic. I have been further illuminated by conversations with certain of Jarrell's critics and contemporaries: Beatrice Hofer, Peter Taylor and Eleanor Ross Taylor, Bob Watson, Fred Chappell, William Pritchard, Suzanne Ferguson, Jerry Griswold, Sister Bernetta Quinn, and Charlotte Beck. Emilie Mills and the staff of Special Collections at the Walter Clinton Jackson Library, University of North Carolina at Greensboro, deserve special thanks, both for their assistance and their hospitality. Thanks are also due my colleagues from George Washington University: Judith Plotz, Bob Combs, and Bob Ganz. The editors of *Children's Literature,* Margaret Higonnet and Barbara Rosen, made invaluable suggestions on the chapter about the children's books which appeared in somewhat different form in their journal. U. C. Knoepflmacher made excellent comments about the article and about the manuscript as a whole, as well as providing inspiration and support in his 1989 NEH Summer Seminar on children's fairy tales. Ron Weber (whose help was above and beyond the call of duty), A. L. Nielsen, David Vancil, Matthew Brennan, and Patricia Pace were instrumental in helping me through their close readings and excellent suggestions. I would also like to thank Charles Adams, Jarrell's first bibliographer, for the gift of some hard-to-find Jarrell items and for bibliographic information on *The Animal Family;* H. Thorne Compton and the Institute for Southern Studies for their invitation to attend the Randall Jarrell Symposium at the University of South Carolina; and Jon Quitslund and the George Washington University for travel funds to attend the conference. The University Research Committee at Indiana State University has supported this project by assisting with permissions fees. The Department of English has given me a congenial place to work and provided me with the assistance of its office staff, particularly Mary Ann Duncan and Mona Dean. I would like to thank Doug Armato and Nancy Grayson Holmes of the University of Georgia Press for their editorial assistance.

Finally, without the support of my family and friends, who read parts of the manuscript and who put up with me while I was working on it, this book would certainly not exist. The following are due thanks far greater than I am able to offer here: Henry Taylor, Ross Taylor, Lilian Weber, Hugh Walthall, Beth Joselow, Cayo Gamber, Margee Morrison, Sera Morgan, Meg Tulloch, Rebecca Brown, Kathy and Rick Merritt-Flynn, Bill and Jane Flynn, Evangeline Pappas, and especially Richard Nicholas Flynn to whom this book is dedicated.

1945, 1947, 1948, 1949, 1950, 1954, 1957, 1968 by Mrs. Randall Jarrell. Copyright renewed 1968, 1969, 1971, 1975, 1976, 1977, 1978 by Mrs. Randall Jarrell. Reprinted by permission of Farrar, Straus and Giroux, Inc.

Randall Jarrell's translations of "Kindheit" ("Childhood") and "Die Erwachsene" ("The Grown-Up") by Rainer Maria Rilke are used with the permission of W. W. Norton & Company, Inc.

ONE

"In thee, thou once a child, in thee"

R andall Jarrell's great subject is childhood, not only in the ways it is experienced and remembered, but in the ways it has been lost and forgotten. In his eulogy for Jarrell, Robert Lowell points out that Jarrell was preoccupied with "how mortals age, and brood over their lost and raw childhood, only recapturable in memory and imagination":

> Above all childhood! This subject for many a careless and tarnished cliche was for him what it was for his two favorite poets, Rilke and Words-worth, a governing and transcendent vision. For shallower creatures, recollections of childhood are drenched in a mist of plaintive pathos, or even bathos, but for Jarrell this was the divine glimpse, lifelong to be lived with, painfully and tenderly relived, transformed, matured—man with and against woman, child with and against adult. ("Randall Jarrell" 109–10)

Although childhood for Jarrell takes on the quality of a transcendent vision, he recognizes its tenuousness, that it is a state imperfectly re-called by memory. Childhood can only be reexperienced through the imagination; recapturing childhood is a complex task requiring persis-tent devotion.

At first, Jarrell approached the task of reclaiming childhood by arm-ing himself as a child. Karl Shapiro says, "With Jarrell . . . the child

becomes the critic and center of value" ("The Death" 223), Lowell in
Notebook calls him "Child Randall"(51), and Eleanor Ross Taylor describes him as possessing "the terrible candor and honesty of a child
—a prodigy" (letter to the author, 8 June 1984); other friends and
critics characterize him as childlike, or even childish. Clearly, Jarrell
was continually aware of his own unusual childhood, one he remembered with "total recall" according to Mary Jarrell (interview with the
author, 12 June 1984). In many ways the origins of his quest were
highly personal, traceable to a childhood characterized by conflict.

Randall Jarrell was born in Nashville, Tennessee, on May 6, 1914,
the second child of Owen and Anna Campbell Jarrell, whose first
child, a daughter, had died in infancy. Randall's parents were quite
young and financially insecure, "two babies with their baby" (Jarrell,
Complete Poems 354).[1] Their marriage was difficult, and they were
separated several times before their divorce in 1926.[2]

As a boy, Jarrell was considered both precocious and charming—
a prodigy and "the darling of older people." But adult approval must
have been ultimately erratic, as he was often shuttled among farflung
relatives upon whom he depended for both financial and emotional
sustenance. Perhaps as solace, or as an attempt to sustain an emotional lifeline, he became an early and avid reader, encouraged by both
his mother and his grandmother, "who read to him all the time." His
mother, Anna, seems to have delighted in his precocity, perhaps to the
point that she exaggerated his accomplishments. "At one year," writes
Anna in her son's baby book, "he played only with books . . . at twenty
months he could repeat in broken sentences the stories of 'Three Little
Pigs,' 'Three Little Bears,' 'Red Riding Hood,' 'Jack & the Beanstalk,'
'The Green Pear.'" Clearly, Jarrell's belief in the transforming value
of tales was deeply rooted in his own early childhood.

Anna Jarrell's baby book demonstrates her enthusiasm and delight
in the infant Randall, but it also hints at the family's instability. In the
first fifteen months of his life, Jarrell's family moved from Nashville
to Louisville, back to Nashville, and then to California, apparently

relying on the kindness of Jarrell's uncle, Billy Pearson, for financial support. Young Randall felt very close to his mother, but their frequent separations throughout his boyhood led him to associate separation with betrayal. He dissociated himself from those he loved the most because he feared losing them, a fear that for the most part seems justified. Though Mary Jarrell says that she "never got the impression that Jarrell's childhood was miserable," she also recalls that when she and Jarrell first met and were discussing each others' families, Randall remarked, "Oh—my family's a disaster."

Yet periods of Randall's childhood appear unusually happy, even idyllic, and the period that seems to have made the greatest impression on him occurred when he lived with his paternal grandparents and great-grandmother in Hollywood—from 1925 through late 1926—while his parents were getting a divorce, the period that serves as the setting for his major poem, "The Lost World." This poem captures the uneasy coexistence of happiness and fear that characterized Jarrell as a child, fascinated by his Hollywood paradise but disturbed by his parents' estrangement.

At first, Hollywood was indeed a boy's paradise for Jarrell, but soon he again experienced betrayal when his mother sent for him to return to Nashville. His bitterness and confusion about the continual loss of family, whether actual or surrogate, is later reflected in "A Story," a poetic monologue spoken by a boy in exile at boarding school. The poem is a truncated sestina, missing its envoi, a form indicative of the abrupt end and sense of loss of his idyllic existence in Hollywood.

Before moving to Hollywood, Jarrell had modeled for the figure of Ganymede on the Nashville Parthenon. Peter Taylor, who was growing up in Nashville at the same time, recalls having heard of Jarrell long before he knew him, both as the boy who had modeled for the figure and as "a boy who knew a lot" (241). Jarrell professed to remember that he had so charmed the sculptors by his storytelling abilities that they actually asked his mother if they might adopt him. In her memoir, "The Group of Two," Mary Jarrell reports that Randall's mother didn't dare tell him. When finally informed, Randall bitterly remarked, "She was right. I'd have gone with them like *that*" (286).

Young Randall felt betrayed, bitter, and confused in 1926 when his mother sent for him to return from Hollywood. The abrupt separation from his grandparents and great-grandmother, combined with the onset of adolescence and the pain of his parents' divorce, created a sense of betrayal so great that Jarrell, a prolific letter writer, never tried to communicate with his lost family until he wrote "The Lost World," long after they were dead. The coexistence of wonder and betrayal, charm and bitterness, would haunt Jarrell all his life.

Jarrell's career as a writer began when he was in high school, and his reputation as a "boy who knew a lot" was certainly deserved. In 1931, when he was a senior at Hume-Fogg High School in Nashville, a fire destroyed his personal library, and he prepared a list of his books for insurance purposes. The list (reproduced in the appendix) includes Proust, Tolstoy, Faulkner, Eliot, Dostoyevsky, Flaubert, Spengler, and Bertrand Russell, among others.

Many of the articles and reviews he wrote for the Hume-Fogg High School *Echo* from 1928 through 1931 show him to be a sophisticated writer as well. One caustic review of a production of *Hamlet* contains Jarrell's assertion that he has memorized the whole play. When he was in junior high and high school he would spend his afternoons in the Carnegie Library waiting for his mother to finish her work as a teacher of business English.

Randall does not, however, appear to have been entirely bookish and solitary. His other interests included acting and sports of all types. Though he felt close to his mother throughout his adolescence, he continued to seek the company of surrogate families, the most important of which was the Breyer family, whose daughter Amy became Randall's first love, and to whom he would remain deeply attached in later life.

Jarrell's family intended that he work in his rich uncle Howell Campbell's candy business after graduating from high school, but because of his lack of aptitude for business and his obvious intellectual promise, Campbell sent him to Vanderbilt, making Jarrell the first in his family to get a college education. At the same time as Randall was entering Vanderbilt, his mother remarried, an event that seems to have disappointed Randall deeply. Indeed, Jarrell experienced a series of domestic betrayals throughout his youth: the loss of his father, the loss of his grandparents, and the loss of his mother through her remarriage. These losses led Jarrell to be extremely reticent about his personal life to all except his closest friends. Recalling his childhood in a 1942 letter to his estranged lover, Amy Breyer de Blasio, Jarrell said

> It's all true about growing up—you'd lived at home, in one place, in the middle of the Biggest Family in the World, and never been alone at all. I've lived all over, and always been separated from at least half of a very small family, and been alone as children ever are. As long as I can remember I'd been so different from everyone else that even trying to be like them couldn't occur to me. (*Letters* 60)

"One of the most obvious facts about grown-ups, to a child, is that they have forgotten what it is like to be a child," Jarrell says in his essay on Christina Stead's *The Man Who Loved Children* (*Third Book* 31). Yet Jarrell seems determined to remember what it's like, trying to keep the promise of the child speaker of "The Lost World": "*I'll* never forget / What it's like when *I've* grown up" (286).

As his career progresses, Jarrell's determination to remember childhood deepens. Of the 154 poems in *Selected Poems, The Woman at the Washington Zoo, The Lost World,* and the "New Poems" section of *The Complete Poems,* over a third concern childhood or children directly. After the mid-1950s, Jarrell's interest acquires new force, perhaps stimulated by the process of translating Rilke. In addition to the many poems, Jarrell's work includes six books for children, all of them completed in the 1960s, four of them original—*The Gingerbread Rabbit, The Bat-Poet, The Animal Family,* and *Fly by Night*—and two of them translations from the tales of Grimm and Ludwig Bechstein. These books coincide with Jarrell's exploration of his own childhood in "The

Lost World," and its companion-piece "Thinking of the Lost World," which were among the poems written during a final sudden burst of activity after a long period of poetic silence.

That Jarrell's increased interest in childhood helped him overcome the feeling that "a wicked fairy has turned me into a prose writer" (Mary Jarrell, "Afterword" 281) is hardly unusual considering the nature of the prose he was writing. Late in his career, childhood became his supreme fiction, a compensatory response to his prescient and pessimistic view of society and the age, best represented by the overtly polemical essays in A Sad Heart at the Supermarket:

> The climate of our culture is changing. Under these new rains, new suns, small things grow great, and what was great grows small: whole species disappear and are replaced. The American present is very different from the American past: so different that our awareness of the extent of the changes has been repressed, and we regard as ordinary what is extraordinary—ominous perhaps—both for us and for the rest of the world. (86)

Jarrell discovers in childhood a way out of this impasse. By remembering childhood that has been repressed, adults collide with the enormity of what has changed in the world around them. By understanding the past, they can gain secure footing and begin to stabilize a society that is rapidly deteriorating. For Jarrell, childhood is the primary emblem of hope in what is a deeply conservative vision.

This conservative vision is not without its challenges or dangers. Jarrell recognizes that the worthwhile past is not readily available in memory, that indeed it is often falsified by it. Rilke says in The Notebooks of Malte Laurids Brigge, "I prayed to rediscover my childhood, and it has come back, and I feel that it is just as difficult as it used to be, and that growing older has served no purpose at all" (65). The adult who manages to recapture childhood finds it, beneath what has been idealized, just as difficult as ever. Certainly, Reinhard Kuhn's observation in Corruption in Paradise: The Child in Western Literature that "the search for childhood paradise leads to its ruins" (120) applies to Jarrell. Though Jarrell is often misread as a poet with a sentimental or idealized view of children, it is clear that he is fully aware of the ruins. The adult, he says, views his childhood "almost as if the grown, successful swan had repressed most of the memories of the duckling's miserable, embarrassing, magical beginnings. (These memories are deeply humiliating in two ways: they remind the adult that he was once more ignorant and gullible and emotional than he is; and they remind him that he once *was*, potentially, far more than he is)" (*Third Book* 19).

Yet what Kuhn says of Rousseau, that he "makes a conscious effort to create a childhood paradise he had never known" (112), could also be said of Jarrell. What disturbs Jarrell most about the changing climate of modern culture is that fewer and fewer adults even attempt to pray for childhood's rediscovery. The loss of childhood becomes analogous to a loss of faith. We tend to idealize the past rather than rediscover it, and so lose access to the present. Jarrell describes the unease that arises when a culture refuses to address its shared past: "When we look at the age in which we live—no matter what age it happens to be —it is hard for us not to be depressed by it," he says in "The Taste of the Age," and even if, a certain number of years after, people "look back at us and say ruefully: 'We never had it so good' . . . the thought that they will say this isn't as reassuring as it ought to be" (*Sad Heart* 16–17).

Jarrell's view of childhood is inextricably linked to his view of society. If children possess the potential that adults have lost, the "new rains, new suns" of the brave new world of modern America become even more insidious than they seem because children, the hope for the future embedded in the present, are their primary victims. The victimized child is a prevalent image in Jarrell's poetry and prose, because it fuses his personal experience with a more universal experience.

The child's victimization is most dramatic in the context of war poems like "The Truth," but it is more subtle and pervasive in the context of postwar America where it is manifested most strongly in education. Jarrell, who taught most of his life at the Woman's College of the University of North Carolina at Greensboro, had an excellent reputation as a teacher, and once said, according to Lowell, "If I were a rich man I would pay money for the privilege of being able to teach" ("Randall Jarrell" 105). His concern for the erosion of educational values is reiterated in essays such as "The Obscurity of the Poet," "The Taste of the Age," "Poets, Critics, and Readers," "The Schools of Yesteryear," and "A Sad Heart at the Supermarket," and most brilliantly, in his novel, *Pictures from an Institution*. It is particularly pertinent that even though the adolescents in *Pictures* seem utterly deprived, the younger children are yet more deprived. It seems likely that Jarrell's interest in writing for and about children is motivated by his concern about the effects of postwar American values on these children.

Speaking to an audience in 1963, Jarrell said that all his poems were about animals, women, and children, and joked that "all the men got killed in the poems I wrote about the War" (*Poetry of Randall Jarrell,* tape). The War and its aftermath seems to have directed the poet's attention to the War's survivors, the traditionally unempowered, who served as an emblem of the future. The child, in particular, is both a positive and a negative emblem. As Jarrell says in "A Ghost, A Real Ghost": "The child is hopeful and unhappy in a world / Whose future is his recourse" (262).

Like the child, Jarrell is both hopeful and unhappy. At the same time he skewers the "supermarket" culture, he wants to win the approval of the very people who inhabit that culture, an audience that his friend Hannah Arendt calls "the television watchers and readers of *Reader's Digest*" (7). Jarrell's social criticism is paralleled by a move to more conversational poems in which the child becomes more and more a central figure. Ultimately, Jarrell senses that he and his audience share a universal predicament, the loss of childhood.

Jarrell's mature work is an effort to speak to that audience by reimagining what has been lost in order to gain what has not yet been won. What seems important in the mature writer is not Jarrell the child, but rather, in the words of Jarrell's translation of Rilke's "Die Erwachsene," Jarrell the "once a child" (*Kindgewesene*). Even his children's books are not entirely *for* children—he calls *The Bat-Poet* a "book half for children and half for grown-ups . . . that felt just like a regular book to me" (M. Jarrell, Liner Notes). The child becomes the center of value for Jarrell because the resurrection of the child's consciousness may restore the adult's access to the sense of wonder and promise experienced by children.

This search for lost childhood is dangerous, however. In undoing repression, the adult must confront the child he or she was, whose beginnings are as miserable and embarrassing as they are magical. In becoming "once a child" (i.e., an adult who retains the accurate memory of childhood) the adult recalls his or her own treatment as a child in which adults represented "the capricious infinite." Because of the widespread mistreatment of children, the adult who manages to recapture childhood discovers, in the words of Jarrell's translation of Rilke's "Kindheit," "knowledge ever harder to hold fast to."

In "The Grown-up" and even more so in "Childhood," Jarrell learns from translating Rilke the nature of the loss of childhood that informs his attempts at rediscovery in the late work. "The Grown-up" depicts the moment that the veil of adulthood descends upon a girl so that she is left with "all her questions":

> All this stood on her and was the world,
> And stood on her with all things, Pain and Grace,
> As trees stand, growing and erect, all image
> And imageless as the ark of the Lord God,
> And solemn, as if set upon a State.
>
> And she bore it; bore, somehow, the weight
> Of the flying, fleeting, far-away,
> The monstrous and the still-unmastered,
> Unmoved, serene, as the water-bearer

Stands under a full jar. Till in the midst of play,
Transfiguring, preparing for the Other,
The first white veil fell smoothly, softly,

Over her opened face, almost opaque,
Never to raise itself again, and giving somehow

To all her questions one vague answer:
In thee, thou once a child, in thee.

(239)

The veil's descent indicates the onset of "adulthood" at the moment of self-recognition, of separateness from the world. Jarrell's version of the poem suggests that one becomes aware of one's childhood only through its sudden loss "in the midst of play." When one truly recognizes childhood, it is seen as frightening and difficult, "monstrous and still-unmastered." Its loss involves self-awareness and discovering one's identity, but the process is seen primarily as something done to the child who in trying to objectify the world ends up objectifying herself ("All this stood on her and was the world"; "And she bore it; bore, somehow, the weight . . . Unmoved, serene."). Though the child is inevitably lost within the adult, she resides within the adult, the "once a child" as the one vague answer to the many questions. For the "once a child" (*Kindgewesene*), childhood remains the source for the true answer, though for most it is a source that is difficult to tap; the means for reclaiming childhood are inescapably "rusty / And hard to move and absurd, a squirrel-wheel / A sick squirrel turns slowly, through the sunny / Inexorable hours" (300).

Mary Kinzie, in her essay "The Man Who Painted Bulls," argues that

Jarrell cannot rehearse the *changes of state* from infant to child, child to adolescent, adolescent to adult. He can only record the sense of confusion *within a state* that has no clue as to how to get itself changed. This is the source of the trapped, bewildered pathos on the part of the child questioning the adult world, the sense of loss of the mature being looking back on the child, and of the dead looking back on the living. Often, Jarrell will insist that the two are one, the man the child, the living the dead. . . . It is further significant that the realm of the early years to which his poetic dreams recur is principally the period of latency, not the earlier precognitive period. It is as if the two great periods of libidinal and aggressive energy, infancy and adolescence, had been erased by their very violence, and what remained were the states among which Jarrell holds his dialogue, childhood and maturity, two periods of achieved quiescence that do not know their real histories or their real name. (833–34)

On the contrary, Jarrell's later poetry and the Rilke poems he chose to translate show that he is primarily interested in the change of state from child to "once a child." Certainly infancy and adolescence were disturbing to Jarrell, but they are hardly absent from the poetry. Even though he had an intense interest in Freud and psychoanalysis, he seems more attracted to the literary, mystical exploration of *changes of state* than to an exclusively psychoanalytic exploration. After getting his bachelor's degree in psychology from Vanderbilt, he pursued graduate studies in English. William Pratt is correct in saying that "Jarrell held the Romantic faith that art could and must take the place of religion" (484). Among twentieth-century poets, Rilke best filled the role for Jarrell of high priest of poetry.

"Childhood" is the Rilke translation that most resembles one of Jarrell's own poems. Though he calls it an adaptation, it is an excellent and accurate translation:

> The time of school drags by with waiting
> And dread, with nothing but dreary things.
> O loneliness, O leaden waiting out of time . . .
> And then out. The streets are gleaming and ringing,
> All the fountains flash up from the squares.
> In the parks the world is enormous.
> And to walk through it all in one's little suit
> Not at all as the others go, have ever gone:

O miraculous time, O waiting-out of time,
O loneliness.

And to gaze far out into it all:
Men and women, men, men—black and tall
And going slowly, as if in their sleep,
Beside the sudden white and blue and red
Children; a house here, now and then a dog,
And one's fear changing silently to trust:
O senseless grief, O dream, O dread,
O bottomless abyss.

And then to play with top or hoop or ball
Beneath the paling branches of the park
Or sometimes, blind and wild in the reeling
Rush of tag, to brush against the grown-ups,
But to go home with them when it is dark
With little stiff steps, quiet, held fast to:
O knowledge ever harder to hold fast to,
O dread, O burden.

And to kneel beside the great gray pond
Hour on hour with one's little sail boat,
Forgetting it because so many more,
Lovely and lovelier, glide through the darkening rings
And to have to think about the little pale
Face that shone up from the water, sinking:
O childhood, O images gliding from us
Somewhere. But where? But where?

(242–43)

Kuhn's reading of this poem is particularly instructive—"Rilke's child is entranced by his own drowning image, and childhood itself becomes a series of evanescent comparisons. It is of such vanishing metaphors that the new music of childhood is composed" (219). Like the protagonist of "The Grown-up," the child in "Childhood," once he becomes aware of himself and the world ("so many more, / Lovely and lovelier"; "the sudden white and blue and red / Children") loses childhood itself; childhood resides "Somewhere," but it is lost within him. As Schiller states in *Naive and Sentimental Poetry*, adults look at the child "from the *limitation* of our condition": "The child therefore is a lively representation to us of the ideal, not indeed as it is fulfilled, but as it is enjoined; hence we are in no sense moved by the notion of its poverty and limitation, but rather by the opposite, the notion of its pure and free strength, its integrity, its eternality" (51).

Yet Jarrell's versions of these Rilke poems, and his own poems about childhood, show that he is aware of the child's poverty and limitation as well as its strength and integrity, and as the Rilke poems show, its eternality is tenuous. In the first stanza of "Childhood" Rilke depicts the child's vague longing for change, his fear, and his feeling that the world (and time) is enormous. From the state where the child sees only adults, "Men and women, men, men—black and tall," he becomes suddenly aware of other children and other objects. With his play he tests the adults' authority by brushing against them, but, in defeat, he goes home with them. If his fear has turned to trust, it is a misplaced trust. His faith in the external world is called into question by the world itself, with so many more objects lovely and lovelier than he'd imagined. The child, unable to escape his feeling of poverty and limitation, finally succumbs to a recognition of self, which, because of the nature of the recognition, causes him to lose himself. He sees that childhood is valuable only as it glides by him, as he changes from *Kind* to *Kindgewesene*. The questions are many, the answer singular and vague: "Somewhere. But where? But where?"

"Childhood" is clearly the central Rilke poem in Jarrell's developing image of childhood. Besides the concept of the "once a child," it also contains the other important "fictions": the impingement of the "enormous world" that Jarrell delineates in his critical writing and the evanescent fiction of the family that will become the central concern of his children's books and of "The Lost World." Jarrell wishes

to see childhood by removing the blinders of the adult, thereby transforming a vanishing metaphor into a supreme one that is potentially
redemptive.

As he would demonstrate many times, the nexus of family is the
primary context for exploring childhood, because in the whirlwind of
American culture, the greatest thing that seems to have grown small
is the family:

> A man on a park bench has a lonely final look as if to say: "Reduce
> humanity to its ultimate particles and you end here: beyond this single
> separate being you cannot go." But if you look back into his life you can-
> not help seeing that he is separated off, not separate—is a later, singular
> stage of an earlier plural being. All the tongues of men were baby-talk to
> begin with: go back far enough and which of us knew where he ended
> and Mother and Father and Brother and Sister began? The singular sub-
> ject in its objective universe has evolved from that original composite
> entity—half-subjective, half-objective, having its own ways and laws and
> language, its own life and death—the family. (*Third Book* 3)

If the child buried within the adult is the key to understanding one's
life, then the adult's search must begin even farther back with that
earlier plural being, the family. In this brave new age where the family
appears to be disintegrating, the poet is forced to create a figurative
family: to adopt one, as it were. "Once a child" Randall, following the
vague promise of the child's consciousness, has created in his poetry
and fiction an adoptive family, one that he hopes will extend to the
reader and make him or her exclaim, "He's right. I'd go with them
like *that*."

TWO

"The Elementary Scene"

D enis Donoghue points out that Jarrell's early poetry "is not his choice work" because "the feeling is raw, and Jarrell was not good with raw wounds" (52), but another explanation for the disappointing early work is simply that Jarrell was still under the influence of his Fugitive mentors. Influenced by his teachers, John Crowe Ransom and Robert Penn Warren, Jarrell decided not to pursue his studies in psychology, but, rather, to take the M.A. in English at Vanderbilt. When Ransom was hired away by Kenyon College, Jarrell followed him there, working as an instructor and rooming with Robert Lowell. Jarrell's original plan to write his thesis on Auden was not approved, so he changed his topic to A. E. Housman, and completed the thesis under the direction of Donald Davidson. But Allen Tate became the most important of Jarrell's Fugitive mentors, one Mary Jarrell describes as a father figure. Though they were to have a falling out over Jarrell's refusal to accept Tate's advice about the order of the poems in *Blood for a Stranger,* Tate's influence casts a long shadow over the early poetry; many of the poems are indebted to either Tate or Auden. Furthermore, most of Jarrell's early publication can be directly attributed to his connections with Tate, Warren, Ransom, or Cleanth Brooks. But if Jarrell's early work owes too much to his mentors in terms of its style, he was already beginning to formulate his attitudes toward childhood. Like the bat-poet, Jarrell would eventually outgrow his need for men-

tors, and rather than writing poems to order, would write them for
himself.

Jarrell's early view of childhood as a clouded battleground between
innocence and experience is rooted in observations of how children
are victimized by adults who are cut off from their own childhoods
through prior victimization. The volumes *Blood for a Stranger* (1942),
Little Friend, Little Friend (1945), and *Losses* (1948) mirror a pattern
of human development from childhood through adolescence to adulthood, a parody of development in which the betrayed child grows into
an unsuccessful adult. The tone of the early work is accusatory, deter-
ministic, pessimistic, even horrifying, charting a human development
where "journeys end / In no destinations we meant" (360).

Fred Chappell's description of Jarrell's attitude toward childhood
seems particularly applicable to these early volumes:

> There is in Jarrell's poetry the longing to belong to some settled, estab-
> lished, and humane order of existence. There is at the same time a
> painful recognition that this order does not, and probably cannot, exist
> in the world that we know. Yet still it ought to exist somewhere; it is
> a necessary Ideal, just beyond the fringes of the terrible Actual. Jarrell
> would like to posit childhood as one part of this ideal order. . . . but he
> cannot do so. Children in the twentieth century are familiarly conver-
> sant with death, and they are a long way from being immortal. . . . All
> the children in the poems—and there are a great many of them—are
> under attack by a world intent on robbing them of the experience of what
> the poet regards as a true childhood. Losing comfort, security, certainty,
> these children look toward their future lives—when they are to have any
> —with bewilderment and sorrow and sometimes skeptical weariness. In
> some near direction or other lies Childhood, but they have been barred
> from it. (23–24)

As Jarrell says in "London," the child "tumbles all unwilling from
the womb / He reaches for a breast and gets a bone" (360). This early
poetry dwells on the "terrible Actual," and despairs of finding a "necessary Ideal." There is a distinct absence of the qualified faith Jarrell
was to find in the later work.

This absence of faith is derived from a world view that perceives no meaningful distinctions between innocence and experience. Robbed of their childhoods and conversant with death, twentieth-century children come into the world not "trailing clouds of glory," but "bewildered and depressed." As Chappell makes clear, Jarrell's modern children *are* outcasts, "and they are a long way from being immortal." The triumph of the terrible Actual renders the modern world entirely adolescent and solipsistic, blurring the boundaries between youth and age, innocence and experience—and ultimately, good and evil. Jarrell, never comfortable with the New Critics' rejection of the Romantics, dissents from the party line in his early essays, "A Note on Poetry" (1940) and "The End of the Line" (1942), and expresses the now commonplace notion that modernism did not reject romanticism, but carried romantic principles to their absurd outer limits, primarily as a result of the fragmentation of society and poetry's tendency to succumb to the fallacy of imitative form.

Almost without relief, the early poetry depicts the child as betrayed and confined, falling from his mother's sleep (a twilight sleep brought on by anesthetics) into "the State." *Blood for a Stranger,* Jarrell's first full collection, is rife with images of the violent fall from the womb into a violent and bloody primal sink of modern, automated, inhumane humanity. "A Little Poem" (circa 1936) contains such imagery, as well as one of few expressions of Jarrell's animosity towards his younger brother, Charles:

> All night in the womb I heard stories.
> My brother was a fish, began, "O fish!"
> And I listened till my gills began to fall.
> There in the dark I leveled my pig's stare
> And warm and wet, my limbs were ripened, and my wit
> Was blood along the bough. "I am done now,"
>
> I said to my brother, he said, "I know nothing."
> So I fell first into this sink of time.

(362)

The speaker is born into betrayal: "The world's word grew like butter on my tongue / I cried to my brother: 'O go back!'" But the speaker is first-born into an awareness that the second child, being blest by indifference and "A dumb wish budding into wives, a house" (363) avoids. Possessing a consciousness which denies him access to that dumb wish, the speaker is haunted by an unfulfillable wish to deny the horrors he sees all too clearly:

> I saw more than I had wit to bear,
> I heard more than I had heart to hear—
> A hand was laid upon me, not my own.
> I saw, I said, *I see it not,* my heart was heavy
> With blood, I heard, I said *I hear it not.*
>
> (363)

Clearly, Randall was upset about Charles replacing him as his mother's favorite; Mary Jarrell says that Randall resented Charles and called him a chronic liar and thief. Jarrell's mother, Anna, was married at age sixteen, and apparently was quite unstable. Abandoned by her husband some time in the early 1920s and left to raise two young boys, she was subject to fainting spells, often boarding her children with better-off relatives. She seemed to swing between smothering her children with affection or ignoring them (Mary Jarrell, interview with the author, 12 June 1984). In his adolescence, according to Mary Jarrell, Randall often went to the movies on Saturday night with his mother, and was pleased when his friends thought she was his date. There is no direct testimony or evidence that child abuse, repeatedly alluded to in the poetry, ever took place, but "A Little Poem," "Variations," and "The Bad Music" (the latter addressed to "You, Anna") depict abusive mothers as metaphors of a horrifying and abusive world.

In "Variations," child protagonists, who bear the names Kipling gave to his own Punch and Judy in "Baa Baa, Black Sheep," convert their mother into a horrid nurse:[1]

> "I lived in a room full of bears and porridge,
> My mother was dead and my nurse was horrid.

I sat all day on a white china chamber
And I lay all night in my trundle bed.
And she wasn't, she wasn't, O not a bit dead!"

The boy said, the girl said—and Nurse she said:

"I'll stew your ears all day, little hare,
Just as God ate your mother, for you are bad,
Are bad, are bad—" and the nurse is the night
To wake to, to die in: and the day I live,
The world and its life are her dream.

(122)

The identification of the child with a murdered rabbit appears many times throughout Jarrell's work; the image of abusive toilet training occurs just this once. Womb and breast imagery is particularly prevalent in the early poetry, but it is usually avoided later on, even in the Rilke translations such as "The Olive Garden" (1948) where the German *Schoss* (literally "lap" or "womb") is translated as "hearts," though the imagery does surface in poems such as "The House in the Wood" (1964). "Variations" begins with a Punch and Judy show and ends with a negative judgment of the world man created, a world that matter-of-factly betrays children:

"I was born in a hut, my wit is heavy.
My sister died, they killed my father.
There is no time I was not hungry.
They used me, I am dying.
I stand here among graves."

The white, the yellow, the black man said.
And the world said: Child you will not be missed.
You are cheaper than a wrench, your back is a road;
Your death is a table in a book.
You had our wit, our heart was sealed to you:
Man is the judgment of the world.

(122)

In a world where man has usurped God's authority, the victor's judgment is terrifyingly arbitrary, bringing destruction to the powerless,
with the child as a paradigm of powerlessness. This world speaks with
the tongues of men only, who are the only actors, and as in the Punch
and Judy show of the first section, also their own managers: "And
'Clap,' said the manager; 'the play is over'" (121).

"The Bad Music" is much more personal, almost hermetic. Although
it is addressed to "Anna," Jarrell confesses in a letter to Amy Breyer
that "*The Bad Music* is certainly your private poem" (Wright 178). The
poem can be seen then as doubly addressed to Amy the disappointing
love, and to Anna the disappointing mother:

> I sit, sit listening; my lashes droop
> And the years come close around me like a crowd
> Of strangers I knew once and they say nothing,
> And I see at last they were never mine.
> The breast opening for me, the breaths gasped
> From the mouth pressed helplessly against my wrist
> Were lies you too believed; but what you wanted
> And possessed was, really, nothing but yourself:
> A joy private as a grave, the song of death.
>
> (367)

The speaker in this poem imagines himself a fool unable either to
laugh or cry. A "mixed-up star" in his emotional turmoil, he is not
sure whether he should love Anna or hate her. The world's confusing
music is "bad"—the speaker knows it is bad—but says, "it's what we
hear." Yet he cannot identify the source of the music: Is it the carollers
outside his window or "the worlds that roll like laughs / To the dark
stream and its immediate sea" or is it Anna who, unlike the speaker,
has "always cried?" Trapped in the undercurrent of unrequited sexual
longing, the speaker tries to identify the source of his predicament first
in his lover, then in his mother, and ultimately, in the world:

> how many know or love at all
> You, Anna? A few so few. Enough.

> This world holds more than we can see or say,
> And it stuffs us like a goose before it kills us.
>
> (368)

With its echoes of *Hansel and Gretel,* "The Bad Music" is Jarrell's attempt to objectify and explain his particular and private pain in terms of "this world," a world that in 1940 was at war, mirroring but dwarfing the merely personal. Jarrell indulges in a hermetic, personal lament somewhat narcissistically in the poem, but for him the stakes are high. Blaming "Anna," but unable to acknowledge his blame, Jarrell transforms the witch, Anna, into the world; rather than having the witch/mother stuff the child like a goose before killing it, he has this world do it. Behind the speaker's confusion over the source of the "bad music" lies his unspoken conviction that the bad music emanates from within himself. He has internalized the pain others have caused him, and though he intuitively connects to a deep source of that pain by naming it "Anna," it is a connection he must shy away from, saying, "Enough."

For Jarrell, at this stage of his career, life itself is diminishment. "Innocence" in a world that makes World War II possible is "worthless as ignorance," akin to American isolationism before Pearl Harbor; but experience, knowledge, and wisdom are also "worthless as ignorance." Though this conflict finds its finest expression in "90 North" (April 1941), it is more explicitly tied to the advent of the European war invoked in "For an Emigrant" (1940). Having concluded that "The world and its life are her dream," Jarrell rejects the merely personal, hermetic lament for the lost love of the abusive mother or horrid nurse, and addresses the 1939 immigrant to America with somewhat didactic pronouncements about that world and its life. He concludes that the dream of the horrid nurse—the world and its life—is a nightmare from which one must consciously estrange oneself; in the words of the prose poem "1914": "It is the dream from which no one wakes" (203).

In Suzanne Ferguson's excellent reading of "For an Emigrant" (*Poetry* 10–11) she notes tellingly, "In the later version of the poem ["To the New World" (1955), *Complete Poems* 80–81] the meanings are less explicit than in the first, and the conclusion is both more muted and less hopeful." Though the earlier version does not seem to me to be hopeful, it is certainly more explicit and less muted. The emigrant, addressed as "Child" throughout the poem, flees Germany and wanders westward, finally to America, a land whose indifference and solipsism are embodied in the image of the Statue of Liberty as a monstrous innocent with eyes that are evil

> As a child's are evil: blind in the unbearable
> Magnificence of bronze; so absolute in their assurance
> Of power and innocence: the statue's eyes.
>
> And what looks timidly from their clear depths
> Is the child's loneliness, his passionate rejection
> Of his own helplessness and pain, the man's
> Denial of knowledge he cannot endure.
>
> (Jarrell, *Blood* 20–21)

The child/emigrant has wandered into "The maze where all of us are wandering: that History / Where nothing is not repeated." As Ferguson says, "The victim is one with the victimizer" (10). But the personal becomes one with the political. For the speaker

> . . . mistress and Mother fuse at last into a face,
> And Time and my father and the terrible finger
> Of all that I cannot face and must adore—
>
> (*Blood* 21)

and this life of denial and helpless adoration itself becomes fused with "The Accuser, the Appeaser, the inhuman Judge." All of these—mistress, Mother, Time, father, the unfaced and adored, the Accuser, Appeaser, and Judge—

> Are Hitler: a separate peace: the real history
> Where there is nothing that can cause except my lies,
> Where there is nothing that can last except my life,
> Where there is nothing. . . .
>
> (*Blood* 21)

Addressing the emigrant again after this reverie, the speaker says:

> *That* is the world
> You must escape from: the America where each
> Can think still, "I am innocent."
> But there is guilt enough for all: existence is guilt enough.
>
> (*Blood* 21)

Although experience seems unbearable, Jarrell says that monstrous, solipsistic innocence is unforgiveable. Interpreting this charge, Ferguson says, "The Christian doctrine of forgiveness is seen as a sop to conscience, a lie, a sin of omission" (10). Yet there is a paradox in the speaker's seeming assertion that the child should accuse rather than forgive, that she should "Understand and blame," since acceptance and forgiveness later become for Jarrell the signs of maturity. Perhaps the speaker, seeing that the Christian doctrine of forgiveness is futile in a debased world, still values it as something to which one should aspire. Unfortunately, in the world of "For an Emigrant," the only transcendence for the child is estrangement from that world; there seems little hope for maturation, for her to gain not only the ability to understand and blame but also to forgive. The child sees that the face of all she cannot face and must adore resolves itself into her own face, "a child's set face":

> "But I am all of them. That face, that world is mine."
> Change, then. Learn what you can, love what you can:
>   when they kill you,
> Let them look into your face and remember your life
> And cry—"You stranger, you damned stranger!"
>
> (*Blood* 22)

The world of "For an Emigrant" is one where God has truly forsaken us, where the price of existence is guilt. Jarrell seems to be saying that the sins of the parents are irremediably visited upon the children. Childhood breeds not perpetual benediction but perpetual estrangement.

And yet, though Jarrell chronicles the "terrible Actual" incessantly and unforgivingly in *Blood for a Stranger,* he also tries to imagine grounds for hope. The child, though abused by Mother, Father, and the world, has "a peculiar gift for pain," and tries to limit that pain through the imagination. Through dreams and tales, children try to escape their parents and "the capricious infinite," the terrible Actual. Unfortunately, in the 1941 version of "Children Selecting Books in a Library," the imagination provides only a temporary respite from the enormous world:

> Their tales are full of sorcerers and ogres
> Because their lives are: the capricious infinite
> That, like parents, no one has yet escaped
> Except by luck or magic; and since strength
> And wit are useless, be kind or stupid, wait
> Some power's gratitude, the tide of things.
>   (*Blood* 15; *Complete Poems* 106)

Jarrell would rewrite "Children Selecting Books" in 1955, and the two versions share this stanza only. In the 1941 version, the route between childhood and adulthood is one-way: the adults condescendingly "know" that children's tales, the "four cures" (alluding to the number of books children are typically allowed to check out of the library) are analgesic "drugs" that

> are not deadening for our diseases
> And only puzzle us: they don't translate.
> How can these games and giants lure them
> To be clerks or us or crazy? to be great?
>   (*Blood* 15)

Children can gain a temporary respite from the primal horrors into which they are born and reside by escaping into "the elementary scene" —the world of games and school and fairy tales. As in "Carnegie Library: Juvenile Division," it is a shrunken world furnished with the little tables and chairs of the children's library, and these, and even the children themselves, are depicted by the first-person-plural speaker as "properties" that are as unseeing as animals.

The adult is not exhorted to reenter the world of the child as in the 1955 version, by dipping "a finger into Fafnir's blood." Rather the adult is told to use memory (or a single taste of memory) to make the strange language of children "sensible," to make the child's peculiarity integral to the child's learning the debased methods of adults. Children will learn to give up their childhood, "To give up their own dilemmas for the great / Maze of The World—to turn in all their gold / For the bank-notes of the one unwithering State" (*Blood* 15–16).

The speakers of the two versions are so different as to make the two versions entirely different poems. The first speaker maintains ironic distance from the adult attitudes of which he disapproves, as if he were exempting himself, as poet, from the rest of humanity; the speaker of the second version is more fully human, as a result of Jarrell's tendency, especially in the later poems, to identify himself "as always / With something that there's something wrong with / With something human" (317). Coming as it does out of a world where forgiveness seems impossible, the tone of the earlier poem is much more accusatory. The short-lived world of the child is something to be gotten over, a skin to be shed in transit to adulthood, and therefore not particularly valuable; childhood is a shadowy world that cannot be even provisionally recovered, one which is "silent, drowned in time" (1935 version of "The Elementary Scene"). Even the prospect that the child may, for a little while, be able to escape the capricious infinite by seeking the cures of fiction or of make-believe, is illusory. Grown-ups use stories to trick children into learning a "method": "their looks are tricked / By our fondness and their grace into a world / Our innocence is accustomed to find fortunate" (*Blood* 15). But, of course, adult innocence is nothing but ignorance—in the province of irony, there is no fortunate fall, only a resignation to the "one unwithering State."

In the first version, Jarrell's children muster their defenses against the unwithering State of adults with small ineffectual gestures. Since Jarrell was later to claim more for the world of the child, it is not surprising that he rewrote "Children Selecting Books" to reflect his later if limited faith in the redemptive power of art, rooted in an awareness of the residual child within each adult. But in the world of *Blood for a Stranger* even art seems a mere defense mechanism; it is not a cure, but rather one more refuge, like the one sought by the boy who speaks in "A Story."

In "A Story," a boy who has been exiled to a boarding school he detests, decides to embrace the school in order to get revenge on his abandoning parents. Ultimately finding that transfer of affection inadequate, he resorts to self-effacement, vowing to make himself disappear. The infant game of peek-a-boo is reenacted in the prepubescent boy's struggle to let his parents go, his struggle to change his forlorn statement in the fourth stanza, "I don't like these boys," into the bravado invoked in the fifth stanza, "I like these boys":

> I liked home better, I don't like these boys.
> When I wake up I think: "It's dark today."
> When I go out these people hardly say
> A word to me, I wrote home I had lost
> My fountain pen, my mail-box is still empty,
> Because they've all forgotten me, they love their
>
> New friends better—if I don't get their
> Letters ever I don't care, I like these boys
> Better than them, I'll write them.
>
> (131–32)

The boy, however, lacks the power to enforce his choices. At home the boy was taken care of; at school, no one pays much attention when he goes out. Now even the better home is an illusion—at home they've all forgotten him. The poem is a truncated sestina, missing its envoi, and because of the pattern of the repitends, it proceeds from "empty" to "empty," reinforcing the emptiness of the boy's existence. Of course, had the poem retained the envoi it would still have ended on the word "empty," but the boy's wish to lose himself necessitates rendering the final emptiness invisible: the boy becomes like Stevens's Snow Man, "and nothing himself beholds / Nothing that is not there and the nothing that is" (10). But of course, the boy can't really annihilate himself —in order to "have a mind of winter," "one must have been cold a long time." His emptiness is actually open-ended—making his bed empty is probably nothing more than a petulant running away. In following the signs and roads, he is an adolescent lighting out for the territory.

Even though he may feel abandoned, unloved, and lost, the child retains a "dream of discovery." Unfortunately, that dream can serve only his childish heart, a palliative before the arrival into experience translates innocence to ignorance, rendering the child's uncharted potentiality worthless. In "90 North," the theme of adult estrangement from childhood finds its finest early expression. The speaker finds his early childhood dream of discovering the north pole "meaningless," "here at the pole of [his] actual existence"(113). The dream of the child has been converted into the dream of the horrid nurse so that it is the child himself that is dreamed: fantasy turns to reality, innocence into experience, the imagined North Pole into "actual existence"— "the world and its life."

It is pertinent to note that "90 North" originally appeared in the 21 April 1941 *New Republic,* following "London" and "Variations" under the collective title "The World and Its Life Are Her Dream" (Wright 232–34). The three poems taken together chronicle the journey of the child from the womb to unsuccessful adulthood in a world "Where people work and suffer till the death / That crowns the pain." In "90 North," the retrospective view of the experienced adult toward the life of the innocent child reduces innocence to ignorance; the child's world is a "Cloud-Cuckoo-Land," and worthless. Any real meaning that the child makes the adult finds meaningless, leading the adult to kill the child within. The child who reached for a breast but got a bone, who was abused and told, "you are bad, / Are bad, are bad" by the horrid nurse-mother, grows up to be the horrid nurse herself, casts out whatever child-self remains by repeating to himself, full of accusation and denial: "darkness," "nothing," and "pain."

Like Cordelia, the child is not to blame for the parent's abuse and neglect. But the abused child is likely to replicate the behavior of the abusive parent when he becomes an adult, and the adult speaker of "90 North" echoes Lear:

> I see at last that all the knowledge
>
> I wrung from the darkness—that the darkness flung me—
> Is worthless as ignorance: nothing comes from nothing,
> The darkness from the darkness. Pain comes from the darkness
> And we call it wisdom. It is pain.
>
> (113)

The speaker, having confronted "the world and its life," has left himself with no choice but self-annihilation. He has made himself nothing in order to escape notice in a world where he feels that he "die[s] or live[s] by accident alone," a world that seems as capricious and abusive as the horrid nurse. To the speaker of "90 North," the world and its life have truly become "her dream," and with the child's potential to grow into his own transcendent dream of discovery foreclosed, he finds himself dreaming horrid life as the horrid nurse. He feels guilt for an existence beyond his control, comes to feel: "existence is guilt enough."

Like the speaker of "A Story," Jarrell found himself in the midst of "boys" he didn't like when he enlisted in the U.S. Army Air Force shortly after Pearl Harbor. One might well say that his army experience and the war poetry it engendered served as pathway out of adolescence for Jarrell, who had begun to build a reputation as the *enfant terrible* of poetry criticism with his vitriolic attacks on established poets such as Conrad Aiken and Archibald MacLeish. Suzanne Ferguson says, "It would be dreadful to say that a world war was necessary to bring Randall Jarrell to poetic maturity, yet to some extent that is true" (*Poetry* 36). If Jarrell's career transcribes a journey from judgmental hostility to empathetic understanding, the first signs of understanding appear during these war years. The earliest letters to Mackie (his first wife) almost condescendingly dismiss the "baby cadets" (76) with whom he found himself at Sheppard Field in Wichita Falls, Texas. Often these letters leave one with the impression of an adolescent trying to act grown up, but doing so childishly. At the same time he indirectly puffs himself up by complaining to Mackie about the ignorance and callowness of his fellow soldiers, Jarrell also thanks her for sending him a copy of *When We Were Very Young*, "the perfect book for the soldier—this soldier anyway" (*Letters* 79).

Critics have often described the soldiers in *Little Friend, Little Friend* as helpless, powerless, and childlike, but it seems to me that Jarrell's soldiers are primarily adolescents. The false security of the elementary scene provides no protection at all in the army. The knowledge the soldiers have gained in school is of little use because "(When we left high school nothing else had died / For us to figure we had died like)" besides "ants or pets or foreigners"; and now "we burned / The cities we learned about in school" (145). The soldiers are forced to become adults before they have been able to understand their childhoods; like "A Pilot from the Carrier" they read in the wake "a child's first scrawl." Throughout the volume, children are victimized, as evidenced by poems such as "Come to the Stone" and "Mother, Said the Child," but the soldiers are both victims and victimizers. In his pioneering essay, "Randall Jarrell's World of War," Richard Fein observes that "the interior hallucinations of the child are central to Jarrell's war poetry. . . . in some fundamental way childhood and war [are] linked" (155); but though he notices astutely that "children throughout Jarrell's poetry are hunched in fear" (154), he fails to recognize that the soldiers are not actual children. Jarrell's soldiers mirror his own struggle from adolescence toward maturity.

The earliest poem in *Little Friend, Little Friend,* "The Difficult Resolution," appeared in *The New Republic* the day after Pearl Harbor. It shares with the poems of *Blood for a Stranger* the theme of the abused child, and seems to come out of the same kind of private pain. The poem's imagery uses the European war as a metaphor of the same

meaningless existence described in "90 North," and it turns on womb
imagery, "horrid nurse" imagery, and murdered-child imagery. The
war becomes a mother, a "great beast," to which the child's response is
death: "The grave is my mother." The speaker identifies himself with
the nameless European dead

> Who existed only that you might lavish
> Your magnificent and unenduring smile
> On the phosphorescence of bathers, the rockets wandering
> Up to the cold galaxy—my own face
>
> Looking and unendurable in the young night
>
> (399)

Seeing the mortar and sentry on the island, surrounded by "the owned
and amniotic sea," the speaker makes the horrors of war emblematic of
his own pain, the pain of having a mother who "gives and takes away
and gives and in the end destroys."

Like the speaker of "90 North," the speaker of "The Difficult Resolution" finds life meaningless:

> Today, the child lies wet and warm
> In his big mother; tomorrow, too, is dumb,
> The dry skull of the cold tomb. "Between?"
> Between I suffered.
>
> (399)

Likening the world to the great beast, the blind mother, and seeing
that the world holds only suffering, the speaker is faced with unrelent-
ing "degradation," "harshness," "agony," and "intolerable / Anguish."
He can no longer deny the wisdom that is pain with his "No, no!"
and decides to accept his powerlessness. He seems to be saying that he
knows he will always suffer, always be abused by a world/mother that
"weeps at [him], not once for [him]":

> Remember what you learned then: that you are powerless
> Except to know that you are powerless, to learn

> Your use and your rejection, all that is destroying you—
> And to accept it: the difficult resolution.
>
> (400)

The speaker, like the children in the war poems, is a powerless victim, but the soldiers have joined and been drafted into an adult world
at war. The world of once-upon-a-time encounters the adult's failure
of will, and succumbs. Rather than admonishing the child to "Change,
then" as he does in "For an Emigrant," Jarrell comes to see the inability
to change as part of the human condition:

> We learned from you [books] so much about so many things
> But never what we were; and yet you made us that.
> We found in you the knowledge for a life
> But not the will to use it in our lives
> That were always, somehow, so different from the books'.
> We learned from you to understand, but not to change.
>
> (99)

Jarrell, who washed out as a pilot, spent the war stationed in the
U.S. as a simulated-flight instructor and a celestial navigation tower
operator, witnessing death only in training-mission accidents. In *Little
Friend, Little Friend* (whose title is an ironic allusion to Kipling's *Kim,*
the "Little Friend of all the World"), the soldiers, caught in a vise
between the worlds of childhood and adulthood, are forced to behave
like adults before they are adults. They revert to infancy during times
of stress, as in "The Dream of Waking," finding both their childhoods
and their futures erased in the violence of war. Just as it is difficult
to see one's own adolescence clearly when one is in the midst of it,
Jarrell, though he identifies with the pain of his fellow soldiers, is not
really able to evaluate their situation, despite the distance afforded
by his non-combatant status. But he does try to record the soldiers'
predicament truthfully and accurately.

Losses (1948) marks the end of Jarrell's early phase, and in that volume he began to gain a mature perspective on the war. The bombings

of Hiroshima and Nagasaki had a considerable influence on his attitude toward the soldiers who died in the war and those who survived
them. In letters to Margaret Marshall and Robert Lowell he expressed
his disapproval of the bombings; writing to Marshall in September, he
says, "I feel so rotten about the country's response to the bombings
at Hiroshima and Nagasaki that I wish I could become a naturalized
cat or dog. I believe our culture's chief characteristic, to a being from
outside it, would be that we are *liars*. That all except a few neither tell
or feel anything near the truth about anything we do. Though even
at that we're not bad enough to deserve the end we're going to get"
(*Letters* 130). In "1945: The Death of the Gods," he expresses dismay
that "the ash of life / Is earth that has forgotten the first human sun"
(183), and concludes that the gods will learn from the men who made
them how to die.

Jarrell's already tenuous faith in divinity was badly shaken by the
war and the horrors of atomic warfare. This loss of faith is described
in one of the finest poems in *Losses,* "Burning the Letters" (1946),
a dramatic monologue spoken by "the wife of a pilot in the Pacific
. . . speaking several years after his death. She was once a Christian,
a Protestant" (158). Death has turned her husband into a child "at
last"; he seems to grow younger, plays "a part / Of accusation and of
loss, a child's eternally" (158). Yet the "child" the husband has become
in death is not quite the shuddering, aging child the speaker has become. She says, "A child has her own faith, a child's," recognizing
at once that faith and childhood are both lost because she has been
left behind to experience "the darkness—darker / With the haunting
after-images of light"; a world where "lives are fed / Into the darkness
of their victory" (159). Left behind to see the dark victory, the woman
lives because of the death of her husband and all the others killed in
the war:

> Bound in your death,
> I choose between myself and you, between your life
> And my own life: It is finished.

> Here in my head
> There is room for your black body in its shroud,
> The dog tags welded to your breastbone, and the flame
> That winds above your death and my own life
> And the world of my life. The letters and the face
> That stir still, sometimes, with your fiery breath—
> Take them, O grave! Great grave of all my years,
> The unliving universe in which all life is lost,
> Make yours the memory of that accepting
> And accepted life whose fragments I cast here.

> (160)

With the death of the gods, the death of her husband, and the death of childhood, the woman is able to live only in "fragments" which she wishes to cast away, to burn with her husband's letters. The darkness of the victory, made darker by atomic after-images, renders personal survival meaningless: "And my own life: It is finished." The woman knows finally that she herself is implicated in her husband's death and in all the other war deaths: "The dying God, the eaten Life / Are the nightmare I awaken from to night"; she becomes, unalterably, "a troubled separate being," a participant in "the death of Man" because she can't help seeing that man has created God and killed Him. By burning the letters, the widow participates in an act of self-immolation that is analogous to humankind's atomic immolation. The saviour she once believed in becomes a bird of prey:

> The child shudders, aging:
> The peering saviour, stooping to her clutch,
> His talons cramped with his own bartered flesh,
> Pales, flickers, and flares out.

> (159)

Because Jarrell no longer thinks of himself so much as a stranger or outsider, but more as a participant, the later war poems in *Losses* are stronger poems than the poems about the perpetually adolescent soldiers of *Little Friend, Little Friend* who seem forced into adulthood unprepared, and regress to infantile states as a defense against the horrors of war. In *Losses,* Jarrell struggles with maturity by looking at the war from the perspective of a man who "did as these have done, but did not die." Rather than separating himself from the horror and duress of humanity, he makes an empathetic leap of faith in which he neither exonerates himself nor denies the real existential pain he observes and feels. The discovery of this empathetic voice leads to his identification with, rather than his condemnation of, that "something that there's something wrong with . . . something human."

The empathetic voice is at work in "Eighth Air Force" (1947), and it is a voice that is far more satisfying morally and emotionally than the condemnatory shrillness that often mars the apprentice work. The image of adolescent soldiers reverting to childishness by "play[ing], before they die, / Like puppies with their puppy" enables the speaker to meditate on the meaning of his, and their, participation in a war so total man has become a wolf to other men:

> If, in an odd angle of the hutment,
> A puppy laps the water from a can
> Of flowers, and the drunk sergeant shaving
> Whistles O *Paradiso!*—shall I say that man
> Is not as men have said: a wolf to man?

> The other murderers troop in yawning;
> Three of them play Pitch, one sleeps, and one
> Lies counting missions, lies there sweating
> Till even his heart beats: One; One; One.
> O *murderers!* . . . Still this is how it's done:

> This is a war. . . . But since these play, before they die,
> Like puppies with their puppy; since, a man,
> I did as these have done, but did not die—
> I will content the people as I can
> And give up these to them: Behold the man!

> I have suffered in a dream because of him,
> Many things; for this last saviour, man,
> I have lied as I lie now. But what is lying?
> Men wash their hands, in blood, as best they can:
> I find no fault in this just man.

(143)

This poem has been well-explicated by a number of critics, notably by Fein, Cleanth Brooks, Suzanne Ferguson, and Frances Ferguson. Indeed, Frances Ferguson's recognition of the implied pun between the homonyms "pilot" and "Pilate" provides a key to understanding the poem. But her conclusion that the speaker's "incorporation of all the possible stationings toward pain into himself is so thorough that moral scruples seem beyond the point" is a misreading. Richard Fein's suggestion that the speaker recognizes himself as "just man," in the sense of "only man," seems more to the point. Far from ending in moral limbo, the poem seems to be about moral affirmation. The speaker who speaks Pilate's words lacks Pilate's position of authority; his dream incorporates the dream of Pilate's wife, as well, who urges her husband to free Jesus. Certainly the speaker is fallen, is a murderer and a liar; he is also profoundly human. Unlike Pilate, the pilot who speaks the poem does not absolve himself of guilt; if he cannot find fault in the "other murderers" it is primarily because he recognizes that he, too, is not without sin.

"Eighth Air Force" is an exploration of the experienced speaker's attitude toward lost innocence—his own and his fellow soldiers'. All are forced to abandon childhood "in the midst of play." The game of Pitch played in the second stanza is a trivial game, not a meaningful one, which Jarrell described in a reading as being "only slightly more complicated than Animal Grab." The soldiers exist in a kind of developmental limbo between childhood and adulthood, and often act childishly in order to evade their adult fear of dying and their adult guilt over being murderers. Not having been allowed to develop natu-

rally, they are caught in the violent adolescence of war, and are forced
into regressive patterns.

As Jarrell says in a letter to Margaret Marshall, "after all, most of
[the soldiers] were kids just out of high school—[I] believe the majority
of such people who died were too young to vote" (*Letters* 134). Already
in a violent stage of development, adolescence, they are transformed
from young men into murderers, from puppies into wolves. The violence of war does violence both to the remnants of their pasts, and to
their promise for the future; they are caught in an eternal horrifying
present in which they lie silently (both in the sense of being prone
and of evading the truth) counting their missions over and over as they
approach their last. Like the drunken sergeant, the soldiers whistle
arias of innocence in vain, trying, unsuccessfully, to regain their lost
paradises. They cannot, like Pilate, wash their hands of the matter;
they must wash their hands in blood like Lady Macbeth, never able to
get them completely clean, so that they are condemned to remembering. The speaker's recognition that, indeed, this *is* war, and "this is
how it's done" does not finally excuse what is done. Recognizing that
as "a man / I did as these have done, but did not die" and refusing
to find fault with the other murderers, gives the speaker the moral
courage to admit to his own flawed humanity. The speaker does not
assert that because war is hell, he and his fellow soldiers are excused
from behaving hellishly, but rather that war is hell, as soldiers they be-
haved hellishly, and they must live with that knowledge all their lives.
To exempt himself from guilt would mean trying to forget by blaming the "other murderers," and the speaker refuses to forget. Rather
than exempt himself from guilt, he admits that he too is "just man,"
"something that there's something wrong with."

When Jarrell turns to the poetry about "Children and Civilians," to
quote a section title in *Selected Poems,* it is with a renewed acceptance of humanity, as one who writes not from the moral superiority
of distance, but from the compromised involvement of a participant.

In "The Märchen" Jarrell argues that we learn from tales and experience that it is necessary "neither to rule nor die," but "to change! to
change!" (85). "The Child of Courts" (1947, later titled "The Prince"),
"Lady Bates" (1948), and "Moving" (1948) chronicle the necessity and
difficulty of change in terms of child protagonists; and though these
poems are no more reassuring than the earlier poems about the fate of
children, they do locate in "the elementary scene" the sources of the
child's intrinsic potential and value. More than the war poems, these
poems pave the way for the psychoanalytical explorations of the later
poetry. Although the children in the three poems are as abused and
powerless as ever, the poet displays a stronger resolve to affirm the life
of the child. The world and its life—the dream of the horrid nurse—is
still omnipotently in relation to the children it sees as merely "trifling,"
but Jarrell is now the child's advocate—he sees children as holders of
a truth that the world tries to beat out of them, sewing up their eyes
like Lady Bates's.

"The Child of Courts," (a much better title than "The Prince" since
it captures the position of a child victimized by his parents' divorce
proceedings) hunches, quaking beneath the covers after his mother
leaves the room, and imagines his father as a spectre that dissolves,
finally, into "Nothing, Nothing!" Attempting to transcend the pain of
being abandoned by both his parents, he tries to throw off the blankets
of his denial:

> I throw off the furs
> And sit up shaking; but the starlight bars
> A vague window, in the vacant dark
> The sentry calls out something, like a song.
> I start to weep because—because there are no ghosts;
> A man dies like a rabbit for a use.
> What will they pay me, when I die, to die?
>
> (97)

The absent father, who has been the boy's protector, has been replaced
by a pet rabbit "they gave me when he—". Recognizing the inade-

quacy of the father-substitute, the child projects his own feelings of inadequacy onto the pet, a pet he knows will die for a use. Though the child tries to throw off the covers, he is imprisoned by the "starlight bars" coming through the "vague windows," just as he is imprisoned by his father's absence. In a state of confusion, he is caught between the demands of warring parents, which have been resolved unsatisfactorily for him by his father's disappearance and replacement by the speechless, powerless rabbit. The child tries to assert his own wishes by throwing off the covers and reaching out, but he reaches only into emptiness—"there are no ghosts." There is nothing to comfort or protect him, not even the spectre of his father, and the child confronts the obviously mortal rabbit. The child ends up feeling that, perhaps, he is even less valuable than a rabbit, that he is "Nothing, nothing!"

"Lady Bates" represents an enlargement of "Variations IV" in which the child protagonist is a victim of racial oppression as well as the whims of adults. Jarrell depicts Lady Bates as an innocent who is told constantly by her adult oppressors, "you are bad / Are bad, are bad":

> The darning needles that sew bad girls' mouths shut
> Have sewn up your eyes.
> If you could open your eyes
> You would see nothing.

>   Poor black trash
> The wind has blown you away forever
> By mistake; and they sent the wind to the chain-gang
> And it worked in the governor's kitchen, a trusty for life;
> And it was all written in the Book of Life;
> Day and Night met in the twilight by your tomb
> And shot craps for you; and Day said, pointing to your soul,
> "This *bad* young colored lady,"
> And Night said, "Poor little nigger girl."
>
>   (26–27)

The speaker of the poem knows that it is useless to say to Lady Bates what the speaker of "For an Emigrant" says—"Change, then."

The oppressors, the adults, have removed her from the world, making all change but the most elemental impossible; in a way, her death is an ironic release since her life had promised her the freedom to have her hair straightened and wait on other people's tables. Beneath this victimization, however, the virtues of "Lady Bates" are quietly proclaimed: the child is always innocent; she is not an accessory to her own victimization, no matter how much the oppressors insist she is. Though the world may say to her, "Child you will not be missed," the speaker's stance opposes, subverts the legitimacy of that world and expresses complete sympathy with its victims.

In "Moving" (1948) Jarrell confronts from a mature perspective the deprivations he himself experienced as a child. The dramatic monologue by the little girl is framed by the adult's evaluation of that monologue. The girl's monologue (ll. 9 through 33) wistfully describes her family's imminent move to another town, simultaneously uprooting the child from her elementary scene. She turns to fantasy to alleviate the pain by imagining that she and her family are "going to live in a new pumpkin / Under a gold star." The girl's "Never again / Will Augusta be the capital of Maine," her disappointment that she will have to leave her "Dear Teacher," and her being uprooted in mid-fall, just before the Thanksgiving pageant, are disappointments she tries to assuage by imagining herself going to another planet where she will live under the gold star she was apt to get for performing well in school. But the speaker in the frame recognizes that the "never again" is more conclusive; the girl is leaving the elementary scene for good:

> The little girl
> Looks over the shoulders of the moving-men
> At her own street
>
> And, yard by lot, it changes.
> Never again.
>
> (94)

The physical details the speaker provides belie the girl's denial of her deprivation. In the image of the girl clutching her cat as she leaves,

Jarrell recognizes that children try to deny the pain others cause them by believing that things will get better, but the pain does not vanish, it is internalized. Things will not get better for the victimized child. The speaker's peremptory "There is not much else" is a judgment he wishes were unnecessary. In "Moving," Jarrell recognizes the omnipresence of a world where children are uprooted, betrayed, abused, and made to feel guilty for things beyond their control, but he also makes his first step toward trying to reverse that destiny by fully portraying the child's innocence, making tangible what is lost. He hopes poetry will help us to change our lives, but recognizes how difficult that change is. He comes to see that accusation and condemnation are not enough, and begins to embark on his search for a prayer of rediscovery, a journey that will have real, if limited, success.

THREE

The Inadequate Comforter

The publication of *Losses* in March 1948 marked the end of Jarrell's apprenticeship, and the year's subsequent events, some of them personally trying, were crucial to the direction Jarrell's mature poetry would take. The year was marked by controversy—in May, Jarrell defended his negative review of Conrad Aiken's *The Kid* in a letter to *The Nation* (see *Letters* 192–95) and in September, twin reviews of *Losses,* a negative one by W. S. Graham and a positive one by Hayden Carruth appeared in *Poetry* magazine. In late June, Jarrell left to teach at the Salzburg Seminar in American Civilization, his first visit to Europe. In October 1948, having just returned from Salzburg, Jarrell wrote to James Laughlin, "Europe had about as much effect on me as the Coliseum had on Daisy Miller" (*Letters* 203). To Robert Lowell he wrote, "My reaction to Europe was roughly this: Had I actually not been there my whole *life?* Why, how'd I get *along?* (Voice is supposed to rise in incredulous wonder.)" (*Letters* 204).

Europe provided a respite from a life in which Jarrell felt "distracted and harassed," and he found himself falling in love with an imagined past he saw as preferable to his real past; he also fell in love with Elisabeth Eisler, an Austrian ceramist and painter who attended his classes. In her commentary to Jarrell's letters, Mary Jarrell states that although they did not become lovers, "out of deference to Jarrell's marriage," Jarrell wrote to Eisler, shortly after returning to the States, "I

can't be anyone's husband but yours" (*Letters* 197). In a November letter to Eisler, Jarrell took stock of himself and his career with a candor
usually reserved for his scathing reviews:

> I think I'll tell you some things about myself as a person. I work hard
> at poetry but put off, or don't DO, many other things; I hate even the
> feeling of having lots of little duties, even if they're quite easy ones. . . .
> You know how I am about people—rather cold to and bored by a great
> many. . . . As you can see, I'm pretty selfish in many ways, especially
> about writing poems. . . .
>
> I lead an odd, independent, unsocial life remarkably unlike most other
> people's lives, the life of someone whose principal work-and-amusement
> is writing, and reading and thinking about things. . . .
>
> I like the feeling of being taken care of, of having decisions made for
> me, of being saved bother. I'm quite optimistic, mostly in order to save
> bother: I accept, dismiss, and forget about bad things that happen as
> quickly and as well as I can. I guess the one great principle of my life is:
> *O, don't bother, forget about it; I should worry.* (Probably this is because I
> have a quite emotional nervous temperament, and naturally tend to do
> the opposite.) . . . for ten years I've been (1) teaching, or being in the
> army, or being in *The Nation,* (2) writing poetry, and (3) writing criti-
> cism, answering letters from magazines, etc. Having all these going on
> at once means one feels distracted, and harassed, especially if one is lazy
> and easily gets feelings of guilt.
>
> Proust says that intelligence and sensibility are rarely accompanied
> by will; and this (if I may immodestly give myself intelligence and sen-
> sibility) is sadly true of me. It's very hard for me to force myself to do
> anything unpleasant or dreary. (If I'm forced to, as I was in the army,
> that's different.) I guess I can sum up my bad points by saying I can't,
> even if I try, be dutiful and make my life careful and methodical and
> unselfish and self-sacrificing. Even if I tried, I wouldn't succeed.
>
> O, and I forgot to say, I am childish in many ways, but this is as much
> good as bad. (204–5)

Jarrell's wish to recapture childhood, along with his painful recognition that this was impossible, is the subject of the first poem in *The*

Seven-League Crutches (1951), "The Orient Express," a poem which uses a number of phrases from Eisler's letters (*Letters* 207–10). The poet's simultaneous sense of wonder at finding a new spiritual home in Europe, and his disappointment that he cannot make it a real home because he has arrived there too late, provide a fitting introduction to Jarrell's watershed volume. The speaker, journeying eastward into the European heartland, is also journeying into the realm of childhood. He looks out the train window in search of that redemptive world, but what he finds is distorted:

> One looks from the train
> Almost as one looked as a child. In the sunlight
> What I see still seems to me plain,
> I am safe; but at evening
> As the lands darken, a questioning
> Precariousness comes over everything.
>
> (65)

From the objective, impersonal voice of the opening sentence, the speaker switches to the first person in the second, and is almost able to look out with a child's eyes, thinking as a child does, that he is safe. But the impersonal voice intrudes again, bringing a "questioning precariousness" to the child's-eye view. He longs to seek refuge "Under the quilt's many colors," but the colorful quilt turns gray with the twilight. The things of the world, "things from a primer," rather than being merely a gray mask covering the real world, are the world. Although the scene outside the train is composed like a work of art, giving the speaker momentary access to the child's perspective, the effect is transitory. Inverting Rilke's "Archaic Torso of Apollo," the speaker finds that art cannot change his life, much less reorder the world: "Behind everything there is always / The unknown unwanted life" (66). "Like any other work of art," the world outside "is and can never be changed." Perhaps, as in "Children Selecting Books," we can forget for a little while, but in the end we remain "to ourselves endeared,"

eventually exchanging all the gold "for the banknotes of the one unwithering State" (*Blood* 16). Rilke's "Archaic Torso," may tell us "You
must change your life," but Jarrell seems to respond that even though
art helps one to recognize the necessity for change, people lack the
power to change.

The volume's next poem, "A Game at Salzburg," clarifies this pessimism. The three-year-old girl in the poem plays with the speaker
"the little game that Germans and Austrians play with very young children. The child says to the grown-up, *Here I am,* and the grown-up
answers, *There you are;* the children use the same little rising tune,
and the grown-ups the same resolving, conclusive one. It seemed to
me that if there could be a conversation between the world and God,
this would be it" (*Complete Poems* 6). The one-sidedness of that conversation echoes Jarrell's translation of Rilke's "The Olive Garden,"
where even Christ can no longer find God, and is left "alone with all
men's sorrows." Awakening to a recognition of self, the child loses the
sense of connection with the world and is left alone among the things
of the world:

> For men beseech: the angels do not come,
> Never do nights grow great around them.
> Who lose themselves, all things let go;
> They are renounced by their own fathers
> And shut from their own mothers' hearts.
>
> (418)

In "A Game," the things of the world are threadbare, the landscape of
postwar Salzburg in ruins. Though there are signs of renewal in the
landscape, of reassurance in the child who plays her Germanic version
of peek-a-boo, the wish of the poet to believe in the possibility of renewal is continually undercut by his sense that God is indeed absent.
With Rilke's Christ, the speaker seems to be saying:

> And why is it Thy will that I must say
> Thou art, when I myself can no longer find thee.

I find Thee no more. Not in me, no.
Not in others. Not in this stone.
I find Thee no more. I am alone.

(417)

In a world where the evidence of modern warfare is all too evident, no one, not even Christ, can mediate the distance between the world and God. Having succumbed to temptation and having lost the ability to "pray," people are reduced to whispering: "In anguish, in expectant acceptance, / The world whispers: *Hier bin i'* " (68). Although the child "has her own faith, a child's" (159), it is insufficient to fill the void within adults who have lost their faith; without parental or divine authority, humans are cast out of a garden already reduced to ruins. Like Franz Joseph Park, the world has shrunk into a camp for displaced persons. The world's anguished, expectant question, asking for God's affirmation, goes unanswered, in a silence that the world's feeble whisper anticipates leaving only the wish that this were not so.

Throughout *The Seven-League Crutches,* Jarrell's rising voice of incredulous wonder meets disappointment. As "The Orient Express" and "A Game at Salzburg" argue, humankind longs to find a spiritual connection with God through nature, but the modern landscape remains recalcitrant. Prayers, unanswered, dissolve into whispers leaving man, like Rilke's Christ, isolated, "alone with all men's sorrows."

Jarrell seeks escape from this predicament, "by luck or magic," through fictions. Without fictions, he argues, we accept being displaced persons, feel that being prisoners of war "iss a privilege" (67). And yet, this idealized view of fiction is subject to the same limitations as an idealized view of childhood. Though fictions may help us cover great distances, we remain in a sense crippled. Rather than seven-league boots, fictions are, sadly, seven-league crutches. Though art may arm the child for a child's wars, it is often sadly inadequate for the adult. Fiction is the

one cure for Everychild's diseases
Beginning: *Once upon a time there was*

> A wolf that fed, a mouse that warned, a bear that rode
> A boy. Us men, alas! wolves, mice, bears bore.
>
>   (106)

The capacity for creating fictions is seen by the modern world as a sickness. As Suzanne Ferguson says about "Seele im Raum," "Jarrell's point is profoundly disturbing: our sickness is more truthful than our health; our dreams and imaginings more real than our substance. To live happily in this world, one must compromise one's awareness of it" (*Poetry* 153).

Indeed, Jarrell feels that mere survival requires compromised awareness. Even children, in victorious postwar America, are not exempt from this process. As the central poems of *The Seven-League Crutches* —"The Truth," "A Sick Child," "A Quilt-Pattern," and "The Night Before the Night Before Christmas"—demonstrate with horrifying accuracy, the horrors of modern warfare are replicated in the fragmentation of families. Jarrell modifies the trope of generalized modernist fragmentation he inherited from his elders by making the position of the child within the family his explicit concern.

Certainly, in Jarrell's view the war was extremely destructive to families. Writing to Elizabeth Eisler in September, Jarrell reveals that "The Truth" was inspired by "a number . . . of case histories in a book by Anna Freud. One child in the book said, 'I'm nobody's nothing'" (Wright 180). Indeed, Freud and Dorothy Burlingham's *War and Children,* documenting their work in the Hampstead Nurseries, provided not only the inspiration but also the dramatic situation and a number of lines for the poem. Their account sheds a great deal of light on the poem; the little girl they describe has been told that her father is not dead, but that he is in Scotland, and will be back after the war:

> [The child], five years old, the other day broke out in the presence of the mother into a triumphant statement. "I know all about my father. He has been killed and he will never come back".
>
>   The mother answered with a fit of anger, closely questioning the child who had told her "such a lie".

The child only repeated: "You have told me yourself through your behavior". But in the end the mother won.

She made the child repeat: "The father is in Scotland and will certainly return".

The little girl repeated the words after her with a sullen expression and had to promise never to say or think it otherwise. The children of this family show the effects of this discrepancy between the truth they know and feel and the legend they are forced to adopt in wild and unruly behaviour and general contempt for the grown up world. (Freud and Burlingham, 140–41)

Jarrell's triumph lies in transforming the material of case-history into poetry, in creating the illusion of artless verisimilitude. Although the monologue was originally in the voice of a little girl, Jarrell decided to make the speaker a little boy (drawing further on another child from Freud's study, "Bertie").

In Jarrell's note to the poem he says that the child who speaks "The Truth" has been confined to a "mental hospital for children" as a result of the air raids on London in which he has lost his father, sister, and pet dog. He has evaded these deaths with his mother's encouragement; a bright child—he had named his dog Stalky after Kipling's stories —he denies the finality of the devastation to his home and family by converting what has happened into a dream. His understandable wish to escape the truth has been compounded by his mother's complicity, her seemingly humane, but ultimately misguided, lie that his father has gone to Scotland and will be back after the war. Thinking that the child is too young to be subjected to the concept of death, the mother overlooks the fact that in wartime London, death is an open secret. The boy, at his stage of development, can't separate dreams from reality; he thinks dreams are in the room with him like the cinema. The mother, overly solicitous and protective, encourages—and to a great extent dictates the content of—the child's fantasies. In the asylum, the child slowly recognizes that the air raids are over, but the war continues —at least for him. Acknowledging that "The war then was different

from the war now," he explains, "The war now is *nothing*." Rather
than reducing the war to a trifle, the child has made himself nothing
in response to the war. The totality of that loss is confirmed by the
beginning of the sixth verse paragraph:

> I used to live in London till they burnt it.
> What was it like? It was just like here.
> No, that's the truth.
>
> (196)

For the boy, the modern world is as empty as his existence in the
asylum. Though the mother has tried to protect him from the truth in
order to spare him pain, she has instead caused him greater pain. Out
of her limitation as an adult, the mother has, in fact, cut herself off
from the boy, is emotionally unavailable to him, and projects her own
feeling of abandonment onto him. Indeed, the mother's seeming act of
compassion turns out to be an act of extreme selfishness; she acts out
her own abandonment by abandoning her child:

> My mother would come here, some, but she would cry.
> She said to Miss Elise, "He's not himself."
> She said, "Don't you love me at all?"
> *I* was *my*self.
> Finally she wouldn't come at all.
>
> (196)

In struggling to confirm his existence despite his mother's denial,
the boy seeks his real mother in dreams. In dreaming, his mother
seems like his mother, but the boy is not satisfied with this compromised reality. In order to face the truth, he must symbolically kill his
mother, asserting his existence that he knows to be real in the face of
her denial of that existence. When his mother brings him a toy dog for
Christmas, he knows it is one more lie she is using to conceal the real
deaths, a token of her own inability to face reality. In asking his mother
the dog's name, the boy is aware that she is attempting to provide a
substitute not only for the real dog, Stalky (and for the dead father and

sister), but ultimately for the real mother who has disappeared and exists only in dreams. Confronted by her continued self-effacement, her perpetuation of the lie, the boy angrily verbalizes his wish that this Other, this false mother, must be killed, and blurts out, "You're not my mother, you're not my mother. / She *hasn't* gone to Scotland, she is dead!" Coupled with his own guilt about surviving, *him*self, when everyone else has "died," the boy's recognition that there is nothing to protect him from the enormous world causes him to strike out at the adults responsible for that world, an act that is also a cry for help— a tearful plea for his mother to become, again, a real mother, to take care of him, rather than shutting him off in an asylum constructed out of her own limitation and self-anesthetizing denial of the truth.

"Ye shall know the truth, and the truth shall make ye free," proclaims Christ on the Mount of Olives (John 7:32), but since Jarrell's Christ, like Rilke's in "The Olive Garden," no longer mediates between the world and God, those who seek the truth must do so with what Geoffrey Hartman calls an "Unmediated Vision." The difficulty of this task when the Father has disappeared, and fathers are notably absent, takes a particular toll on children. The resourcefulness of the boy in trying to trick his mother into awareness, in trying to force her to acknowledge the truth, is just that—resourcefulness. The child is forced to draw on inner strength beyond the natural stage of his development; if he is to transcend the limitations of adults, it must be by luck or magic. In "The Truth," it is the child who ends up taking care of the parent, even in the difficult resolution of the poem when the mother and son embrace tearfully. Though the end of the poem has been read as a sign of hope signalling a reunion between mother and child, this reading overlooks the poem's underlying bleakness. The boy does not find his mother in this mother; rather, he recognizes that this mother *was* his mother but is no longer. Jarrell's own italics underscore this point, just as his italics underscore the boy's feeling that he alone possesses a "self." The tears at the end of the poem are tears of mourning, not tears of joy. Both the mother and the child are inconsolable, left alone with "all men's sorrows," without the authority of either God or their filial bond.

Jarrell depicts children in a state of sickness and deprivation. Unable to rely on parental or divine authority, they are forced to draw on resources beyond their present capacities for understanding. Though "The Truth" and the earlier poems about children directly affected by the war are more dramatic, the prewar and postwar children who inhabit his later work confront similar situations. Attempting to come to terms with truths beyond his or her capacity for understanding, without divine or parental aid, the child becomes emblematic of the modern, and perhaps the human, condition. But the child's unusual resourcefulness becomes for Jarrell an emblem of hope for modifying that condition. Jarrell seems to be saying that understanding the world is beyond the capacity of adults also, but children are superior to adults because they alone have the strength or wisdom to discover a way out of despair. Perhaps childhood, as a state nearer to the unconscious mind, is a better position for tapping the resources of the unconscious. Since most adults in growing up reject the child's heightened capacity for drawing on the inner life along with rejecting the powerlessness and humiliation of childhood, Jarrell seeks to resurrect the child's consciousness as a possible cure for the age's prevailing illness.

"A Sick Child" is the first poem in the section entitled "Children" in *The Seven-League Crutches,* and the first poem in the section entitled "Dream-Work" in *Selected Poems.* The poem shows the lonely child turning to fantasy in an attempt to escape his mundane, oppressive existence. In an imagined conversation with the postman, the child imagines that the postman brings him letters

> saying everything
> That I can think of that I want for them to say.
> I say, "Well, thank you very much. Good-bye."
> He is ashamed, and turns and walks away.
>
> If I can think of it it isn't what I want.
> I want . . . I want a ship from some near star

To land in the yard, and beings to come out
And think to me: "So this is where you are!

Come."

(53)

The child's parents are absent, and he resorts to an adoption wish similar to the adoption fantasy Freud describes in "Family Romances," except that, rather than replacing his parents with royalty, he replaces them with the twentieth-century American version of royalty—extra-terrestrials.[1] But even extraterrestrials "won't do" because the child has been able to imagine them. What the child misses is the unimaginable, a higher authority, a deity that cannot be expressed in religious terms since he lives in a world that denies the existence of God. The child wants God, of course, but he is able to conceive of Him only as an absence. He expresses his true wish in the terms of an unanswerable prayer: "All that I never thought of—think of me!" The child, playing the same game as the Austrian children in "A Game at Salzburg," receives no "resolving, conclusive" answer. The absence of reliable, responsible authority robs his childhood of meaning, undermines his innocence, even before he is old enough to confront the full import of the absence.

Following "A Sick Child" in both *The Seven-League Crutches* and the *Selected Poems,* "The Black Swan" shows the child turning to fantasy to escape another kind of absence, the death of a sibling. In the poem, the child, unable to accept the finality of death, evades her sister's death by turning it into a fairy tale. Yet this sort of romancing too is sadly inadequate. The child recognizes, whispering as the world does in "A Game": "It is all a dream." Unable to find her sister in reality, the child can find her only in dreams, only by herself becoming, in a sense, dead. Though she has been able to transform her sister into a swan, no leap of faith will bring her back to life. Resurrection is inverted into the possibility that, by dying, and transforming herself into a swan as well, she may become reunited with her sister.

The modern world, Jarrell says, denies children pathways for addressing their difficulties except on the unconscious level of dreams. A wholly secular version of the imagination, however, proves inadequate. Children, denied belief and innocence, have experience thrust upon them before their time. Explaining his distaste for Mahler's *Kindertotenlieder,* even though Mahler was one of his favorite composers, Jarrell says, "The trouble with *Kindertotenlieder* is that it sounds as if those children had always been dead" (*Letters* 268). Jarrell wants to assert the value of his humane view of childhood, one that is essentially Romantic, and he despairs of the modern denial of the child's innocence, continually confronting that denial in his poetry. If there is *life* to be found anywhere in the twentieth century, that life is to be found in the innocence of childhood, and our destruction of that innocence is, for Jarrell, the most shameful aspect of our fragmented, secular culture.

Jarrell's distaste for the *Kindertotenlieder* stems from the same impulse that leads him to revere *Four Quartets.* His criticism of *Kindertotenlieder* is part and parcel of his criticism of twentieth-century culture in general: documenting the triumph of *Thanatos* is meaningless unless one posits an alternative. What is most disturbing about our culture, Jarrell argues, is our unwillingness to let a little child lead us. We not only remain aloof, but we trivialize the life of the child, conspire to destroy it, and then trivialize its death. We operate on the assumption that childhood is dead to begin with.

The child's question in "Come to the Stone," "Tell me why I died" (190), is a question to which the children receive no adequate answer. Their only remaining defense against adult betrayal is a secular, inadequate retreat into fiction, imaginings, and dreams. The child, unable to separate parental from divine authority, confuses the two, and parents come to seem either smothering and overly solicitous or completely absent and unaware. "A Quilt-Pattern," one of the most-explicated of Jarrell's poems (explicated most significantly by Jarrell himself in a letter to Sister Bernetta Quinn), shows more fully than any other Jarrell poem the child's increasing need to hold the destructive tendencies of adults in abeyance.

In "A Quilt-Pattern," Jarrell once again resorts to *märchen* (fairy tales) as a metaphor of our century's destructiveness towards childhood and innocence, and again, the quilt or comforter plays a central role in protecting the child. Significantly, the pattern stitched on the quilt is the "Tree of Life" not the "Tree of Knowledge." And yet, the prelapsarian comforter, for the child in the poem, in the modern world, is an inadequate protector. Like the quilt in "The Orient Express," it grays as night descends, transforming a representation of *life* in its many colors into a shroud, a mere shadow of what it was. Twilight dominates it despite the child's wishes. Parker Tyler, in his seminal review-essay on *The Seven-League Crutches,* observes that the title may be a pun on "guilt-pattern" (143), and an examination of the quilt-comforter image in Jarrell's poems suggests that the quilt represents a kind of security blanket, a false reassurance powerless against encroaching knowledge.

As Jarrell points out in letters to Hannah Arendt and Sister Bernetta Quinn, "A Quilt-Pattern" is the boy's "translation," in his dreams, of *Hansel and Gretel.* But it is more than a "translation" because the circumstances of the boy's life are profoundly different from the circumstances of the protagonists in Grimm's tale.

As in "A Sick Child," the protagonist of "A Quilt-Pattern" "would rather be sick." This boy has not been entirely abandoned by his parents, only by one, his father (cf. *Letters* 303). His mother "has made the child her whole emotional life" (*Letters* 304), and the child, who does not understand his father's absence, feels oppressed by this doting mother who has devoted her day to telling the boy tales. The resemblances between the mother-child relationship in this poem and that in "The Truth" are striking, but the differences are equally pronounced. In "The Truth," it is the secret of *Thanatos,* set against the backdrop of war that the child at least partially understands, that is kept from the child. In "A Quilt-Pattern," it is the secret of Eros that is hidden, and that provides the key to the father's absence. The boy can imagine no rational explanation for his father's absence other than the unconfronted possibility that his Oedipal wish has been realized. The normal Oedipal conflict has, of course, been aggravated by his parents' divorce; and he has been particularly attracted to *Hansel and Gretel* in his dream because it provides him with a loving father he lacks in real life, with a sister/ally he does not have, and with a mother who is truly wicked rather than a mother for whom he has complicated, uncomfortable, sexual feelings.

But the boy cannot escape his particular reality, even in dreams. His dream is a distorted version of *Hansel and Gretel* in which the boy and his mother are the only characters. The good and bad characters manifest themselves as aspects of either the boy or his mother: "good me" and "bad me," "good mother" and "bad mother," "dead mother" and "living mother," "Mother" and "Other," and "boy" and "Other." The boy falls out of the Tree of Life, the faded, inadequate comforter, "into the oldest tale of all." *Hansel and Gretel,* the poem suggests, replicates the oldest tale of all, that of the Fall in *Genesis.* Unlike Adam, however, the boy does not accept a bite of the apple: knowledge is forced upon him entirely against his will. The boy compares the death of his favorite pet, presaging the death of the pet rabbit in "The Lost World," with his own premature awareness of the secrets of sex and death, secrets which elude and overwhelm him. He has a premature awareness of, and a premature sense of responsibility for a world

> Where the cages are warmed all night for the rabbits,
> All small furry things
> That are hurt, but never cry at all—
> That are skinned, but never die at all.
> Good me, bad me
> Dry their tears, and gather patiently
> Through the loops of the chicken-wire of the cages
> Blackberries, the small hairy things
> They live on, here in the wood of the dream.
>
> (57)

To be hurt without crying out is what is expected of the boy. He has been asked by his mother to repress hurt, guilt, questions, longings, has been asked to become, in effect, a caretaker despite his still profound need to be taken care of. His mother's solicitous caresses are for her own comfort, not the boy's, and their ambiguity contains a hint of sexual abuse. In his dream, the child tries to fight off his mother's attempt to consume him emotionally, to force him into the role of re-placing her absent husband. It is not, then, surprising that the boy identifies himself with the murdered pet rabbit:

> Good me, bad me
> Sits wrapped in his coat of rabbit-skin
> And looks for some little living thing
> To be kind to, for then it will help him—
> There is nothing to help; good me
> Sits twitching the rabbit's-fur of his ears
> And says to himself, "my mother is basting
> Bad me in the bathtub—"
> the steam rises,
> A washcloth is turned like a mop in his mouth.
>
> (58)

In this passage, the mother either punishes the boy for becoming stimulated during his bath, for being dirty, or else she vents her anger for her husband's abandonment and her own seduction of the child. Whichever way one reads it, the child is victimized sexually, and one can't help trusting the boy's account of sexual abuse in the dream; the violence done to the boy is made explicit by the images of basting, and the particularly violent punishment of his mouth being washed out with the washcloth. As Alice Miller argues in *Thou Shalt Not Be Aware,* "the child is always innocent," and cannot be the cause of his or her own victimization. The boy in "A Quilt-Pattern," about six or seven years old, is beginning to lose his baby teeth, and has not quite lost the "rabbit's-fur of his ears" that one commonly associates with the infant; he is exposed to an erotic connection with the mother that cannot be dismissed as Oedipal fantasy. In the dream, the boy kills his mother (not his father), though it is too frightening for him to accept responsibility for the death. Upon awakening, all he can do is pretend to be asleep in a talismanic effort to ward the abusive mother off. "Bad me" and "Good Me" smile at each other knowingly and "timidly," unwilling and unable to accept responsibility for the mother's murder, and blaming "the Other"; without the protection of his dreams, the boy numbs himself, pretends to unawareness:

> But they are waking, waking; the last stair creaks
> Out there on the other side of the door
> The house creaks, "How is my little mouse? Awake?"
> It is she.
> He says to himself, "I will never wake."
> He says to himself, not breathing:
> "Go away. Go away. Go away."
>
> And the footsteps go away.
>
> (59)

The "go aways" echo, of course, the boy's attempt to evade the true meaning of the dream, in the dream, when he repeats three times, "I don't know" with increasing emphasis, only to have his mother goad him with the sexual innuendo, "Goose! Goose!" The abused child in "A Quilt-Pattern" has had the secret of Eros thrust upon him by his parent, and though he tries to muster his defenses, he remains defenseless, able only to retreat into numbing denial. Despite Jarrell's desire to make the sexual symbolism unexplicit, that symbolism is what the poem turns on, what makes it so horrifying: "Later (very unexplicitly —I wanted to have it far under the surface, uneasily present) there is a sort of sexual symbolism, since the child does at first conceive of sexual things in terms of his mother, and his mother has made this child her whole emotional life" (*Letters* 304). One feels that the difficulty of this subject for Jarrell is what leads him to want to defuse the sexual aspect; yet, almost despite himself, it is explicit enough.

In her annotations to Jarrell's letters, Mary Jarrell says that "The Night Before the Night Before Christmas" was "the first of Jarrell's semi-autobiographical poems that culminated in the three-part *Lost*

World" (*Letters* 191). The poem is important because it confronts directly the period of adolescence. Adolescence seems to be a difficult subject for Jarrell, as Mary Kinzie suggests in "The Man Who Painted Bulls," and in "The Night Before . . ." he distances himself from the teenage protagonist in three ways. He writes the poem in the third person, alters the gender of the child, and places the poem in 1934, somewhat later than his own early adolescence. The use of female personae offered Jarrell a way of objectifying his experience, and though he had used female protagonists and speakers in *Losses*, notably in "Moving" and "Burning the Letters," most of his dramatic monologues in women's voices were written after 1948, when "The Night Before . . ." was composed. Most likely, writing about the sexual confusion of children and adolescents served as a prelude for Jarrell's later use of opposite-gender personae in his poems.

In any event, several correspondences buttress Mary Jarrell's suggestion that "The Night Before . . ." is semi-autobiographical. In the protagonist's "little family," the sexes of the members of Jarrell's family are reversed: rather than a little boy living with his mother and without his father, the fourteen-year-old girl in the poem lives with her father, and her mother is dead. The family in the poem also includes a younger brother and an "aunt." The brother, as we shall see, plays a central role, but the aunt is conspicuously peripheral. She seems to have been enlisted by the widowed father, who is depicted as rather inept, to help care for the children; yet she does very little, and one detects that the term "aunt" may be a euphemism for the new sexual partner of the single parent. The aunt assumes some of the role of stepmother, in providing the father with companionship, but she rarely acts maternally toward the children. Jarrell himself, of course, was trusted to the care of aunts and grandparents when his parents were getting divorced, and the confusions of identity and sexuality that resulted from this are explored more fully in the *Lost World* sequence. But these confusions, though sublimated, are very much a part of "The Night Before . . ." and surface in conspicuous ways such as in the

adolescent crush the girl has on her teacher, reminiscent of the crush
Louisa has on Miss Aiden in Jarrell's favorite "unread book," Christina
Stead's *The Man Who Loved Children*.

The oxymoronic name of the girl's home—the "Arden Apartments"
—signals in the very first line the tensions between the paradisiacal
life of the child and life in the modern world which is beginning to reveal to the child the secrets the grown-ups share—the world of work,
sex, money, and death. The girl has been told, in the condescending
way grown-ups have of talking to children, that her mother "two years
dead," looked more like a sister, and the child's recollection of this in
a dream intensifies her confusion about the role she plays in a family
that seems no longer to be a family. Furthermore, the girl is becoming
aware of her "self" in ways that are disturbing to her: in her awkward
attraction for her new teacher, in her difficult relationship with her
dying brother, and in her confusion about her own body. The girl

> trails toward the house
> And stares at her bitten nails, her bare red knees—
> And presses her chapped, cold hands together
> In a middy blouse.
>
> (40)

The girl's recognition of her childlike hands and knees, which she
tries to conceal in her fashionable and "grown-up" middy, disturbs her
and is meant to disturb the reader, who discovers through the patient,
unfolding narrative that the girl has had adult responsibility given to
her before she is ready.

The younger, sickly brother confuses his sister with his mother just
as the grown-ups have, and looks to her for reassurance, for answers
to his questions about the existence of God. Beginning to read the
Marxist and proletarian literature of the 1930s in an effort to understand her feeling of alienation from the frightening world, the girl is
caught between childhood and adulthood. On one hand, she attempts
to remain a child in a warm family by getting out the dominoes for a
family game, but on the other, she appears to be her brother's primary

caretaker—serving him dinner on a tray, and reading him his bedtime story. Though she would like to enlist her brother as an ally against the enormous world by reading him Jack London's *The Iron Heel,* the boy, still a young child, would rather hear the decidedly un-Marxist *Stalky and Co.* Though the girl would prefer to read the London—and indeed attempts to shame her brother into letting her by reciting the grown-up admonition, "When I was your age . . ."—she relents, still feeling resentful for having been cast in the role of parent against her will,

> And reads about Regulus leaving, full of courage,
> For that nigger Manchester, Carthage.
> She reads it, *That Negro Manchester,*
> But it's just the same, he doesn't understand.
> She laughs, and says to her brother:
> "Engels lived in Manchester."
>
> The boy says: "Who was Engels?"
> She says: "Don't you even remember *that?*"
>
> (42)

After she puts her brother to bed, she looks into the mirror in her room, in uneasy admiration, like the stepmother in *Snow White,* feeling anomalous, anachronistic. In her confusion between the child-self lost too soon, and the adult-self arriving too soon, she is unable to figure out who she really is. Then, after noticing the anachronistic objects of her childhood:

> Some dolls and a letter sweater
> And a beige fur bear,
> A Pink and a Golden and a
> Blue Fairy Book, all, all in a row,
> Beam from the light, bright, white-starred blue
> Of the walls, the clouding curtains—
> Anachronisms
> East of the sun and west of the moon
>
> (42)

she wraps a copy of *The Coming Struggle for Power* for a girlfriend. *The Coming Struggle for Power,* aside from being as Jarrell's note tells us, "a book, once well known, by John Strachey," is a sign to the girl of her own coming struggle for power against her repressive home life, a struggle she rehearses by ridiculing her father's memberships in the Lion's Club and Moose Lodge, as well as the simplistic mottoes that hang in his office. She thinks, "People are so *dumb,*" and "Why, he might as well not be alive . . ." (43).

Recognizing her failure of sympathy for the unusually distant, "dumb" father, the girl recalls that "Still he was sorry when my squirrel . . . / He was as sorry as Brother when my squirrel . . ." But the uprush of sympathy brings a failure of nerve; the girl cannot finish her sentence because death is too frightening for her to accept. She backs down from her wish that her father were dead, from the recognition that her mother is dead, that her squirrel is dead, and that her brother is dying. Although she tries to comfort herself with "an uneasy, rocking, comfortable tune," Brecht's "Praise of Learning," her confused and increasingly sleepy thoughts, gruesome scenes of child labor, and childish fear of the dark conspire to make her cry "the tears of pain, / Of her own passive, guilty, useless pain." The girl converts Brecht's "LEARN it MEN of SEVENTY" into a recognition that she is, like the child laborers, expected to grow up too soon: "LEARN it MEN of SEVEN"; and that she alone must take care of herself: "WHAT you don't LEARN yourSELF you don't KNOW" (44).

Afraid of this painful truth, she thinks of her brother again, thinks of him dying when he is still too young "Not even to know / Enough not to believe in God." Facing her awareness of the world's injustice and the personal injustice she has had to accept, she thinks "her old worn thought, / By now one word," a resounding NO: "But How could this world be / If he's all-powerful, all-good? / No—there's no God." Brecht's refrain in "Praise of Learning" returns to her in her attempt at personal resolve: "YOU must be READY to take POWER!" (45). But as she gets sleepier, the girl takes off her grown-up mask with "Rexall's

Theatrical Cold Cream," reverts to pre-aware, presexual childhood by donning her "boy's blue silk pajamas" and climbing underneath the inadequate comforter:

> She lies half-in, half-out of moonlight
> In the sheer cold of the fresh
> Sheets, under the patched star-pattern
> Of the quilt; and curled there, warms a world
>
> Out slowly, a wobbling blind ellipse
> That lengthens in half a dozen jumps
> Of her numb shrinking feet,
> Steadies . . .
>
> (46)

Like the boy in "A Quilt-Pattern," she descends into a deathlike sleep in which she tries to make sense of her difficult life in her dreams. The girl's dreams combine all the elements of childhood dreams encountered in the earlier poems: grief over the death of pets, parents, and siblings; the disappearance of God, and the child's attempt to replace God through the use of secular myths, sciencefiction, and *märchen;* and, most frighteningly, the child's recognition that she has been abused—("But you won't hurt me will you? *Will you?*"; "There is something deep / Under her will, against her will, / That keeps murmuring to her, 'It's so.' "; "Dumb, scared, malicious pain"; "The abyss that is her home")—culminating in the tripartite denial, "I don't know, I don't know, I don't know!"

In the dream, *Hansel and Gretel* again plays a significant role. But unlike the boy in "A Quilt-Pattern" who uses the tale to try to resolve his Oedipal feelings, the girl in "The Night Before . . ." uses the tale to try to resolve her confusions in her role as sibling and premature parent. Because the girl, like all Jarrell's children, lives in a broken family in a modern world where wishing no longer does any good, the tale does not resolve the child's problems effectively. The details of Hansel looking back for his white cat and white pigeon in the Grimm's story are transformed into the story of Lot's wife in which looking back turns one into salt. Although the dream cannot alter her world, it allows the girl to see her situation more clearly: to recognize that her brother is dying, and by extension, to acknowledge the other deaths she has denied. Though in her waking hours the girl has tried to convince herself that she must be ready to take power, her dream tells her that she is really still powerless, abused, helpless. United with her dying brother in the dream, she flies with him, looking down at the earth to see that "There is not one bread crumb." The girl's recognition of her brother's impending death is too much to bear: she knows she is unlike Gretel in that she is powerless to prevent her brother's death. She knows also that she is like Gretel because her inability to prevent her brother's death foreshadows a psychic death of her own. She converts her earlier admonition, "When I was your age" to "When I was alive." The pain and deprivation, and premature responsibility inflicted on the girl have led to an effacement of "self" just at the time in her development when she is trying desperately to define herself. Holding her brother's hand, she is unable, like Gretel, to lead him home because home has become a mere whisper of the wind. She becomes a pillar of salt, slowly dissolving in uncontrollable tears.

"The Night Before the Night Before Christmas," like the other poems about childhood in *The Seven-League Crutches,* shows a devastated world, one where divine authority has ceased, so that the possibilities of tradition, art, and fiction meaningfully telling us "You must change your life" are severely crippled. But Jarrell still wants to believe in the power of the seven-league crutches to help us cover great distances despite our infirmities, and says, quoting the father of the afflicted child in the gospels: "Lord I believe, help thou mine unbelief." Continually confronted by modern distortions of our great myths—in which Sleeping Beauty is hacked to pieces and left in a locker in a train station ("La Belle au Bois Dormant"); in which the prince, rather than rescuing the sleeping princess, lays himself and his sword down to join her in death ("Sleeping Beauty: Variation of the Prince"); in which people wallow happily or haplessly in ignorance and denial like "A Girl in a Library"—even this faith in the power of art is severely tested. Our religion, art, and tradition seem broken and fragmented, like the broken families to which our children belong—or, rather, don't belong. *The Seven-League Crutches* represents Jarrell's first real step toward assessing the damage of a modern world devastated by two global wars, and his first real step toward attempting to rediscover tradition, art, and religion, in order to reconstitute out of the ruins a family of children, women, and men.

FOUR

Pictures from
an Adolescent Institution

In "The Obscurity of the Poet," an essay published in 1951 when Jarrell was beginning to write his only novel for adults, *Pictures from an Institution* (1954), Jarrell laments that

> Boys who have read only a few books, but a great many comic books, will tell one, so vividly that it is easy to sympathize: "I don't like books because they don't really show you things; they're too slow; you have to do all the work by yourself." When, in a few years, one talks to boys who have read only a few comic books, but have looked at a great many television programs—what will *they* say? (*Poetry and the Age* 19)

Anticipating the full effects of television on culture, still nascent at the time, Jarrell used the novel as a means of criticizing electronic culture, while also reaffirming human resiliency in the face of cultural adversity.

For all its underlying pessimism and cultural satire, *Pictures* remains, sometimes despite itself, a remarkably affirmative novel. It is humorous, but rarely ill-humored as some of the essays tend to be, and it affirms a high-Romantic conviction that, despite victimization by adults, the child is indeed "the critic and center of value" (Shapiro 220). Jarrell believes that childhood is indeed an exalted state, that the

family is a humane and exalted institution, that we dissolve the boundaries between adult and child at our peril, and that, despite the effects
of mass culture, childhood will continue to exist because it always has
existed. Despite our efforts to the contrary, Jarrell says, a little child
shall lead us.

Pictures is often seen as a roman à clef, or as Peter Taylor has
said, "mainly a book of Randall's witty talk." But it is also a book in
which, Taylor hastens to add, "we see what serious places [Jarrell's]
witty talk could take one" (250). During an extended discussion about
the differences between European and American values, the character Irene Rosenbaum delivers the telling observation, "You Americans
do not rear children, you *incite* them; you give them food and shelter and applause" (180). While characterizing that statement as one
of the "familiar cliches of European settlers in America," the narrator
nevertheless acknowledges its essential truth.

In her essay "To Benton With Love and Judgment," Suzanne Ferguson notes that *Pictures* is an articulation of Jarrell's "deeply conservative" standards (276). And undoubtedly, the standards that the novel
articulates herald a growing and highly polemical conservatism on Jarrell's part. By the late 1950s, Jarrell was regularly skewering "modern"
American culture, issuing a series of indictments that culminated in
the essays collected in *A Sad Heart at the Supermarket* (1962).

Jarrell's later essays in particular anticipate the writings of Neil Postman, Marie Winn, and others in the 1980s about the disappearance of
childhood in the United States. Tellingly, such jeremiads, particularly
Postman's, assert that the United States is at the forefront of childhood's disappearance because "America is the first and, at present,
the only culture living entirely under the control of twentieth-century
technology" (Postman 145). Although Jarrell's polemical essays anticipate these currently popular criticisms of mass culture, *Pictures*
is a more convincing indictment of misguided progressivity, largely
because it is never so reductive.

Fred Chappell and others have pointed out that Jarrell's particular views of childhood stem from his wish to believe in the Romantic version of the Edenic myth, modified by the truth that twentieth-century technology has made it difficult for us to believe in that myth, particularly as it concerns children. The novel's fictional institution, Benton College (modelled on Sarah Lawrence where Jarrell taught for a year), represents a false Eden in which children are deprived of their childhood and adults are deprived of their maturity. In fact, Benton seems to encourage perpetual adolescence, an arrested state of development that Jarrell became painfully aware of during the War. Adolescence, as Jarrell defines it in his poetry, involves the illusion that we live in a continuous present, one without either history or hope for the future.

Benton College is the product of a society that has hopelessly blurred the distinctions between youth and age. Presiding over the college, President Dwight Robbins, though ostensibly acting *in loco parentis* to the adolescent girls, is himself an adolescent—a "boy wonder. . . . he possessed, and would possess until he died, youth's one elixir, Ignorance" (16). Although one suspects he would be lost at the helm of a more traditional institution, he is supremely well-suited to be President of Benton College, which encourages, indeed one might say requires, arrested adolescence: "he believed what it was expedient for the President of Benton College to believe. . . . President Robbins was so well adjusted to his environment that sometimes you could not tell which was the environment and which was President Robbins" (10–11).

Encouraging the whims of narcissism, Benton has few classes—most of the teaching is done in individual conferences—and its philosophy of education is founded on the principle "that one gets more out of one's reading and conversation at college than one gets from college itself":

> Benton decided, with naked logic: Why not let that reading and conversation *be* college, and let the students do ordinary classwork on the outside?—if they felt they needed to; for some of it might profitably be disregarded, all that part that is, in President Robbins' phrase, *boring*.

So the students' conversation and reading and "extra-curricular cultural activities" and decisions about Life were made, as much as possible, the curriculum through which the teachers of Benton shepherded the students of Benton, biting at their heels and putting attractive haystacks before their even more attractive noses: they called this "allowing the student to use his own individual initiative." (84)

Ironically, this flight from pain and effort is disconcerting to the students. As the narrator observes at one point, "The fathers have eaten Cream of Wheat and the children's teeth are set on edge" (20).

Suzanne Ferguson states, "Postwar America is seen in microcosm in the world of Benton College, where social consciousness and self-development are stressed at the expense of scholarly discipline and aesthetic standards" ("Narrative" 73). Although Benton is indeed a microcosm of postwar America, its awareness is skin deep. Without discipline and standards, development and consciousness are impossible. Adolescents become indistinguishable from adults; they have no figures of authority to serve as models for moral development. The morals of Benton are decidedly those of its President: "He had not evolved to the stage of moral development at which hypocrisy is possible. To him the action was right because it was his—he had never learned to judge his own act as though it were another's. If he had told you that he would do something he did it, unless there was some reason for him not to do it. He had the morals of a State; had, almost, the morals of an Army" (72).

One might be tempted to add that he had the morals of a child, for even "the freshmen of Benton thought the President younger than they. (Though they themselves were as old as Time, and wondered when the grown-ups—the other grown-ups—would see that they were)" (15). But one would be mistaken. The President, and by extension his institution, tend toward an amorality mediated only by slogans because they have not reached the maturity that makes both morality and hypocrisy possible. Unable to tolerate growth, Benton resists whatever threatens to disrupt its complacent, static, and perpetual adolescence. The personal is seen as idiosyncratic and ill-adjusted, and only by maintaining its homogeneity can Benton survive.

Jarrell's major argument in *Pictures* is that the family, an inherently conservative institution, is our only vehicle to escape the uniformity that pervades our culture. But the family must be reinvented, transformed. In *Pictures,* Jarrell poses the existence of the ideal, adoptive family in the figure of Gottfried and Irene Rosenbaum's adoption of Constance Morgan, set against a host of dysfunctional families pervading the novel. The Robbinses, the Whittakers, and the "group of one and a half"—Gertrude and Sidney—are all dysfunctional or incomplete families as well as essential cogs in that quintessentially dysfunctional family, Benton College. The dysfunctions of Benton and its member families are acute narcissism and solipsism, qualities that undermine any developmental model of human life. The Institution itself can be rendered only through "pictures" because its life is a frozen pose. Despite its reputation for being "progressive," Benton is remarkably set in its ways, remarkably impervious to the outside world. This static artificiality extends to many of Benton's most prominent figures. As Jarrell admits in a letter to John Crowe Ransom, most of the less sympathetic characters are "types": Robbins, for instance, is "just a type, inhuman because he is no more than a type," and "Gertrude reminds people violently of five or six lady writers" (*Letters* 366–67). Benton's students, too, are mostly undifferentiated: "girls who had read Wittgenstein as high-school baby-sitters were rejected because the school's quota of abnormally intelligent girls had been filled that year. (The normality of the intellectual environment at Benton was rigorously maintained)" (80). Indeed, to the child/critic John Whittaker, the girls of Benton are not human at all, "they're androids" (271).

Jarrell's major criticism of these "types" is that they lack humanity, an indictment stated most explicitly in the narrator's estimation of the visiting novelist, Gertrude Johnson:

> Gertrude had one fault more radical than all the rest: she did not know— or rather did not believe—what it was like to be a human being. She was

one, intermittently, but while she wasn't she did not remember what it had felt like to be one; and her worse self distrusted her better too thoroughly to give it much share, ever, in what she said or wrote. If she was superior to most people in her courage and independence, in her intelligence, in her reckless wit, in her extraordinary powers of observation, in her almost eidetic memory, she was inferior to them in most human qualities; she had not yet arrived even at that elementary forbearance upon which human society is based. (190)

In satirizing Gertrude, Jarrell resists part of his own nature as a critic, in which his early condemnation of other poets' weaknesses was partially inspired by his need to mask his own frailty. This passage anticipates Jarrell's essay about Christina Stead, "An Unread Book," in which he says that most adults have forgotten what it is like to be a child. The narrator of *Pictures* informs us that "one scrap of childhood remained to [Gertrude], the feeling that everything is absurd" (43). In Gertrude, one sees personified the Jarrellian paradox about the gulf between children and adults. This paradox rests on the principle that childhood is indeed a separate state, the memory of which must be retained in order for the adult to be a successful human being; but at the same time, childhood is a state that must be transcended through one's development, and this development is primarily moral rather than merely cognitive or intellectual. Gertrude is a superior intellectual being, entirely successful in everything but "human qualities." Her superiority becomes crippling because she does not identify herself as a human being, evidenced particularly in her novels, the last of which, entitled *These Mortals,* is mean-spirited without the leavening of puckish delight or forgiveness. If the narrator develops morally to the point that he suffers fools gladly, Gertrude merely finds fools insufferable.

In addition, we see clearly in his attitude toward Gertrude the narrator's ambivalence about his impulses to judge and to love, a dialectic Suzanne Ferguson treats at length in her essay "To Benton With Love and Judgment." Contrary to Karl Shapiro's assertion that the less sympathetic characters in *Pictures* are "immolated," the narrator insists on identifying the humanity in characters who themselves reject humanity. No matter how much characters like Gertrude Johnson and President Robbins may reject humanity, they are blessedly unable to erase their own human frailty. Gertrude's misanthropy does not extend itself to her relationship with her husband Sidney, and even President Robbins is a character Jarrell admits in his letter to Ransom that he rather likes: "As you'll see later in the book I rather like Robbins, and think about him, 'Poor creature, if only he could become more human!'" (*Letters* 367). The failure to be *more* human is a failure of scale. Characters mistakenly believe that institutions are larger than individuals rather than the exaggerated caricatures of individual human qualities they are. That is, individuals embody all the complexities and contradictions of human nature, while institutions, as products of human invention, represent a narrowing of that range of qualities. Gertrude observes of President Robbins, "That's no man, that's an institution," and it is precisely the drive to become a Benton person that turns its keepers and wards into something less than human. But Jarrell the novelist, like Jarrell the poet, insists upon identifying himself "with something that there's something wrong with / With something human."

The failure of Benton, and of postwar America, is their drive to achieve an "abject ordinariness." Although Jarrell has a qualified faith that "in the end everybody turns off the television set; and looks up at the stars in perfect silence, or starts an FM station to play Bartok, or prints Rilke in a paperbound book, or plays with his cat, or throws kisses to his wife, or does something ill-adjusted, individual, and personally satisfying" (*About Popular Culture*), he nevertheless sees how our society narrows the range of choices needed to become individual and fully human. That narrowing of choice is most frightening when it erases the awareness of the possibility of choosing. Indeed, one sees that Jarrell's criticism of postwar America is centered on the ways in which the child is increasingly confined, in which the child's highest aspiration is to become ordinary. Although there are only three actual children in *Pictures,* the atmosphere in which they are reared is far from salutary; one of the most noticeable things about their upbringing is the amount of energy their parents devote to not noticing them. The children react to this indifference by developing such salient characteristics as growling or becoming obsessed with snakes. Only the narrator seems to exhibit penetrating concern for the children. He alone understands their unusual defenses and sympathizes with their intent to maintain their individuality despite adult attempts to suppress individuality.

The first child the narrator notices is Derek Robbins; and, in relating how Derek is cured of his growling, the narrator reveals himself as a critic of the unnecessary curtailment of children's natural impulses. Derek, at nineteen months, has not yet begun to talk, so his mother Pamela takes him to a child psychiatrist—"no Freudian, but a homely, American, social-worker sort of psychiatrist" (18). Derek doesn't talk, but he does growl at people, and this makes him, in the narrator's eyes, extraordinary: "he had a wonderful growl, an astonishingly deep growl for so young a child—and unless you had a heart of stone you growled back. Not even Lotte Lehmann has made sounds that have bewitched me like that growl: when I heard it I not only believed in the Golden Age, I was in it—I felt for a moment that life was too good for me" (19).

But the narrator, after an absence from Benton, comes back to find Derek transformed into a "drearily ordinary child." The narrator recognizes, however, that Derek's ordinariness is itself "a kind of defense against his world and its two pillars, Dwight and Pamela—he had been taught to call them by their first names" (20). Furthermore, there are moments when he sees under the shell of Derek's ordinariness: "I heard his mother reciting him a fairy tale before he was sent up to bed; he made her repeat all the parts of the story in which giants or dragons or step-mothers were killed. He seemed to need these repetitions: that commonplace little boy by the sandpile was only Derek's imaginary playmate" (20). Despite moments like these when Derek's "crust of ordinariness" is lifted "as the hood of a car is lifted," he has, by becoming "just a dopey little boy," made himself "almost ideally disappointing" to his parents; Dwight and Pamela encourage his dreary ordinariness. Thus, when Derek comes out of his shell, he does so in ways that seem ill-adjusted to "normal" adults:

> At the nursery school children painted and modelled and cut out; and Derek was different from the others, from the beginning, in one way— he painted, modelled, and cut out nests of snakes. By the end of the year he had improved a great deal: the snakes in his paintings were smaller, and pushed down into the left-hand corner of the paintings, next to the feet of a big little boy; he modelled cows and bears, though their legs *were* snakes, and he pasted his cut-out snakes into links, and made a construction-paper chain out of them.
>
> The nursery teacher asked me despairingly: "Now what, may I ask you, is the prognosis for a child like *that?*" The growls and snakes—and Derek—had made me like Derek so much that I hated to say it, but I replied, "I guess he'll turn into a grown-up in the end, one just like you and me." The teacher said, "But I'm not joking"; and I said to myself, "But I'm not joking." But what both of us meant to say was, I think: "Poor little boy! poor little boy!" (20–21)

The prognosis for the children of the Benton faculty is not good. Not only will they turn into grown-ups in the end, but, one suspects, into unusually neurotic grown-ups. Either the children will recede into the dull complacency of their parents, or, if they happen to be unusually precocious like John Whittaker, they may become artists or scientists. More frighteningly they may become monsters like Fern Whittaker whom the narrator describes as "a proto-Fascist." In her generally excellent essay on *Pictures*, Suzanne Ferguson finds the children "gratuitously implausible" ("To Benton" 281), but I would argue that they are central to the theme Ferguson identifies as that of the lost or false Paradise. If we take Derek to represent the norm in that he will probably turn out to be ordinary and disappointing, we see in the Whittaker children the polar extremes of the monstrous and the prodigious child. It is far from gratuitous that the boys in *Pictures* are both obsessed with snakes; it seems only natural in their reaction to the debased Paradise of Benton for them to invoke the serpent. As the narrator speculates, snake-obsession is most likely endemic to Benton children: "In my whole life I had known only two children who drew snakes, John and Derek Robbins; both were Benton children. Sometimes I wondered uneasily about this, and wanted to ask the other parents at Benton whether their children drew snakes" (56).

While Derek is subjected to living under the shadow of those two pillars, Dwight and Pamela, the former childishly egocentric and the latter characterized by her Boer racial stiffness, John and Fern Whittaker are subjected to living under the distracted authority of their highly comical parents Flo and Jerrold. The older Whittakers are characterized by their absentmindedness and their devotion to public rather than private life. If there are characters in *Pictures* who might be described as gratuitously implausible, then the Whittakers are prime candidates. Flo Whittaker is "surely the least sexual of beings; when cabbages are embarrassed about the facts of life, they tell their little cabbages they found them under Mrs. Whittaker" (46). Flo exhibits insensitivity to almost anything not approved by *The Nation,* and she is particularly insensitive and unattuned to her children. When her son John (inspired by science fiction, "not the kind in which a man rescues a girl from a big extra-terrestrial being who is about to do Heaven knows what to her, but the kind in which you have described to you the civilization of organisms that utilize in their metabolic cycle, instead of oxygen, fluorine, methane, or ammonia") says, "Mother, I dreamed I was married to a girl with blue blood," Flo answers, "We Americans don't believe in things like that any more, dearest" (56). As the narrator observes trenchantly, Flo "cancelled out a half-a-dozen good Republicans" (59). Her babbling husband, Jerrold, an admired professor of sociology, is even more unaware of what goes on around him, and seems even more oblivious to his children's eccentricities.

Just as Benton students may occasionally excel despite their education, John Whittaker is able to excel despite his parents. To emphasize the long odds against that achievement, this silver lining is deliberately withheld till the end of the novel. What we encounter early in the novel is the terrifying side of parental neglect manifested in the character of the youngest Whittaker, Fern. According to the narrator, Fern is "as people say, a Little Manager; Fern wanted, as people say, Her Own Way. (That was all she wanted, but it was enough: the Milky Way was small beside Fern's)" (57). Although this monstrous child should alert the Whittakers to their failings, they remain oblivious: "Fern was a thorn in the flesh to remind the Whittakers that they had flesh; but they weren't reminded" (57). Like the other inmates committed to Benton, the Whittaker adults are not only disembodied but lack spirit, something that provokes their children to develop spirited, and sometimes not altogether savory, personalities to avoid their parents' homogenization.

In "A Sad Heart at the Supermarket" (1960), Jarrell says, "True works of art are more and more produced away from or in opposition to society" (84). And if we accept, as I believe Jarrell would have us accept, that successful families are like true works of art, we come to see that true families are more and more produced away from or in opposition to society. In *Pictures,* the analogy between the family and the work of art is made explicit, and it seems to have replaced Emerson's infant as the perpetual messiah; Jarrell would have families and works of art come into the hearts of fallen men to plead for a return to paradise. The narrator of *Pictures* has not only the twin impulses of love and judgment, but he has split feelings about his relationship to society. This ambivalence reflects Jarrell's own when he qualifies his statement in "Sad Heart" about the production of true works of art: "And yet, the artist needs society as much as society needs him: as our cultural enclaves get smaller and drier, more hysterical or academic, one mourns for the artists inside and the public outside" (84). Like the narrator, Jarrell is "a living—still living—contradiction": as an artist he must produce in opposition to society, but the effect of that work must register within society. Quoting Ernest van den Haag in "Sad Heart," Jarrell asserts, "One may prefer a monologue to addressing a mass meeting. But it is still not a conversation" (84). Though *Pictures* punctures society's illusions through caricatures, Jarrell also genuinely attempts to initiate a conversation with that society. To facilitate that conversation, he alleviates the novel's satire with compassion and empathy. As Ferguson points out, "even his 'worst characters,' Gertrude Johnson and President and Mrs. Robbins, are allowed at least touches of humanity and affection" ("To Benton" 273).

Jarrell's compassion is located in his portrait of the old-maid teacher of creative writing, Miss Batterson, an innocent who reveals Jarrell's ambivalent attitude toward the Romantic view of childhood:

> One can hardly help being primitively attracted to the Romantic belief that potentiality is always better than actuality, that Nothing is better than Anything; yet looking at Miss Batterson, one could not help doubting it. . . . Miss Batterson was potentially everything and actually almost nothing. She was still, after so many years, taking her first look at life; that first look was her vocation. She had made trembling-on-the-verge-of-things a steady state, a permanent one: she lived in the State of Innocence. (92)

Yet exaltation of the prelapsarian is insufficient both for Miss Batterson and the rest of us in fallen postwar America; Benton, rather than nurturing children with an eye toward encouraging development, neglects them, allowing them to remain statically, adolescently "on the verge." Miss Batterson is allowed to remain untouched by human hands, like one of the hilariously failed sculptures in the "Art Night" section. A kind of explanation for Miss Batterson's refusal to enter the state of experience is offered retrospectively. The narrator's memory of Miss Batterson, who has died before the events of the novel take place, is centered on her story of a particularly Jarrellian boy in a tree house. The face of Miss Batterson's father, hunched in fear in his tree house, watching his animals being killed by Union soldiers, resolves itself into "a child's set face"—Miss Batterson's face.

Although he would agree with Irene Rosenbaum that "Nostalgia is the permanent condition of man" (162), the narrator is finally unable to accept nostalgia as a cure. He at once admires and deplores innocence, and sees the family as the mediator between innocence and experience. But Benton is not a family, and within Benton there are no families that fulfill their mediating function, at least not natural families. When the narrator finds the adoptive family of the Rosenbaums and Constance, he must accept that such families are exceptional, in all senses of that word.

Constance Morgan (modelled after Jarrell's long-time younger friend Sara Starr) is an exemplary innocent; she seems to the narrator "a fairy tale" (151), and it is through a fairy tale, "The Juniper Tree," that she eventually begins to recognize the necessity to grow up. Constance has been an orphan since she was fourteen, motherless since she was five, and because she has been deprived of the mediating presence of a family, has been sheltered and has sheltered herself against growing up. The Rosenbaums have been sundered from their family and their country by the war and the Nazis. Constance represents to them "*really and truly* . . . all that a daughter would be for [them] if [they] had a daughter" (261). Recapturing the unfulfilled opportunity of creating their own family, they are allowed the possibility of passing the traditions of their lost European world on to Constance. Nevertheless, they know this creation is only temporary; "It is only for a little while," says Irene, "a daughter is nothing to keep. Someday in a year, or two, or three she will want to be a grown-up" (261–62). The narrator— himself displaced, orphaned in the sense that he is a poet, "a maker of stone axes"—wishes, "joyfully, 'Don't you want to adopt me too?'" (262). But the narrator lacks Constance's "dreamy absent innocent style." Unlike Constance he is no longer "ripe for the Rosenbaums," and can see that the Rosenbaums have faults, that they are human.

Recognizing that the family exists as a figurative construct as well as a natural one, Irene jokes that they adopted him long ago.

Constance, though she appears ordinary, is actually extraordinary, in her potential and innate humaneness. The narrator knows that "the person who treated Constance as a girl like any other girl would have treated Cezanne as a painter like any other painter" (146). Having lost her family, "She had been somehow sheltered from things; and when she hadn't been she had managed, like a sleepwalker, to shelter herself without ever seeming to. Later on what she already knew would recur to Constance, and this time it would be transmuted: life is, so to speak, the philosopher's stone that turns knowledge into truth" (147). Her adoptive family will help her grow. Although the narrator often wishes that "change and chance and choice [would] *leave her alone*," he knows that it is inevitable that she will taste of the tree of knowledge. And he is heartened that her passage will be eased by her reconstituted family of Gottfried and Irene.

Because of the Rosenbaums' decision to adopt her, Constance is able to begin to confront knowledge. In reading Grimm's "The Juniper Tree," she encounters what she has been avoiding all her life—the painful loss of her family, particularly her mother, which becomes felt through the work of art. Reexperiencing her loss through the mediating form of art, Constance reads of the mother's death in childbirth, "and when [the mother] beheld [the child] she was so delighted that she died," and begins to weep uncontrollably. The veil of Constance's repressed childhood begins to dissolve in those tears, but beginning to confront what has been lost does not, by itself, make the loss understood: "The story was to Constance in some way her life, but there was something else that she did not understand; and she wept in joy for herself and her happiness, and in grief for her own stupidity and the world's. The story held for her the tears of things, and she murmured in childish—or, perhaps, human—anguish: "Oh I wish I had more *sense!*" (265).

It is Constance's good fortune to be entrusted to the care of the Rosenbaums, who will help her understand. With the wisdom of tradition behind them, and a surer knowledge of "the tears of things," the Rosenbaums offer Constance acceptance, nurturing, and the promise of her own adulthood. They will not fix her as an eternal child; she is to remain with them only until she grows up. Indeed, the Rosenbaums offer to Constance what is offered to few: a chance to find, not "a child's set face," but her own face. True families, Jarrell argues, are all adoptive; adults should be caretakers rather than owners of their children.

But since there is no longer any possibility to find his own adoptive family, since he has long been cast out into the world, the narrator must make "a separate peace" with that world—with Benton. Having made his preparations to leave Benton for good, the narrator takes a stroll through the campus and is confronted by two emblems of hope. The first is in the form of a child, John Whittaker, who serves as a mirror for the narrator. The narrator recognizes not only John's unusual intelligence, but sees his own unfulfilled youthful wish to be a physicist (and one might add, Jarrell's own youthful preoccupation with science fiction). This encounter with the child as emblem of hope is a lucky prelude.

In restoring his faith in the human spirit, the narrator's encounter with his boyish other makes him receptive to another miraculous emblem. He is summoned by the art teacher Sona Rasmussen—whom he had thought a "potato bug" and about whose sculptures he'd felt, "It's ugly, but is it Art?"—to see her newest creation, a sculpture made out of unpromising materials: a railroad tie that "had been fixed so that it revolved, like a weather-vane, on the brass rod that supported it." And from an unpromising artist working with unpromising materials has come a real work of art, one reminding the narrator of essential humanity: "The railroad tie had become a man, a man who floated in the air as the foetus floats in the womb; his pressed-together arms and legs, his hunched-up shoulders, his nudging face were indicated in broad burnt lines or depressions, so that you could hardly tell whether the man had been drawn or modelled: he was there" (274–5). The sculpture is entitled "The East Wind," and the narrator recognizes that it is, indeed, the East Wind. Seeing that this "potato bug" has been "visited by an angel," he vows from then on to "suffer potato bugs gladly." The narrator has been led by a child, like a child, to a discovery about humanity "by luck or magic." He is able to accept with equanimity the fallen and still fallible world around him. Feeling both the joy and "the tears of things," he is able to reenter the world, reassured by a measured faith in the potentiality of the human spirit to create something from what appears to be nothing.

FIVE

"Alas! Eternity"

T*he Woman at the Washington Zoo* (1960) represents an attempt by Jarrell to circumvent his poetic silences. Particularly during the last half of the 1950s, he found it difficult to write poetry, complaining to Mary, "A wicked fairy has turned me into a prose writer" (Mary Jarrell "Afterword" 281). Paradoxically, Jarrell's poetic output declined just as he was achieving eminence in the world of letters. *Pictures from an Institution* was a best-seller, going through four printings within a year; his *Selected Poems* appeared in 1955 to substantial acclaim, and he was appointed Consultant in Poetry at the Library of Congress in 1956, a position he was to hold until 1958. The consultantship led, as it often does, to an increased demand for Jarrell as a lecturer, and he was continuing to build his by now legendary reputation as a great teacher, evidenced by projects such as *The Anchor Book of Stories* (1958). One is tempted to note an element of self-criticism in his admonition to Robert Lowell about "91 Revere Street," a prose poem included in *Life Studies* (1959): "But it's not *poetry,* Cal!" (*Letters* 416).

Perhaps the 1950s were prosaic times for Jarrell's circle. Berryman's biography of Stephen Crane appeared at the beginning of the decade; Elizabeth Bishop was publishing short stories in *The New Yorker* (she would wait her characteristic ten years between poetry collections); and, primarily as a result of Lowell's aborted attempt at writing his prose autobiography, the delay between *The Mills of the Kavanaughs*

(1951) and *Life Studies* was nearly as long as that between Jarrell's *The Seven-League Crutches* and *The Woman at the Washington Zoo*. Certainly in Jarrell's estimation the decade was profoundly disturbing, despite its superficial blandness. For Jarrell, the Eisenhower years were years in which "Fred Waring [was] in the White House" (*Letters* 449), years in which

> The doors shut themselves
> Not helped by any human hand, mail-boxes
> Pull down their flags, the finest feelers
> Of the television sets withdraw.
>
> (227)

Of the nineteen original poems in *The Woman at the Washington Zoo* the latest is "Jamestown" (1957); only four poems were composed in 1956; in 1955, the year of *Selected Poems*, Jarrell published no poetry in magazines whatsoever. Seven of the nineteen poems were written between 1951 and 1955, and the remaining seven before 1951, the date of *The Seven-League Crutches*. By contrast, most of the translations in the volume appeared in the years 1956 through 1960.

Jarrell had come to see Americans, like the woman at the zoo, as "beings trapped" in "dull null / Navy." It is not the woman at the zoo alone who lives a "manless, childless, fleshless existence," but all Americans living in a world where there is no distinction between adults and children, where flesh and blood itself disappears, where we are no longer "helped by any human hand," where we lose our humanity and become "aging machine-parts" (*Sad Heart* 160–70). While the sick child of *The Seven-League Crutches* wants a spaceship to land in his yard and extraterrestrial beings to come out and telepathically tell him where he is, Jarrell himself feels almost as if he were a being from another planet, alienated from a culture hostile to poetry, and ultimately to humanity.

As "Windows" (1954) indicates, Jarrell felt himself alienated from adults and children alike. The speaker of the poem has been seen by critics such as Helen Hagenbuchle as being "obviously a child" (78).

It is more accurate to say that the poem's speaker is neither child nor
adult, but an "adult-child" to borrow Neil Postman's terminology (98–
119). In fact, the speaker of "Windows" resembles the disembodied "I"
floating above the children in "The Elementary Scene" (1960 version);
he is akin to the speaker of "A Ghost, a Real Ghost" (written in 1945),
someone who

> could not believe
> That it was possible to keep existing
> In such pain . . .
>
> .   .   .   .   .   .
>
> Has no need to die: what is he except
> A being without access to the universe
> That he has not yet managed to forget?
>
> (262–63)

The universe from which the speaker of "Windows" is cut off is
the universe of family life, which is only barely discernible through
windows in "the lights of others' houses" (232). Like the speaker of "A
Girl in a Library," he knows that, unfortunately, "the ways we miss
our lives are life" (18). The life that exists inside the other people's
houses has fragmented into "portions of a rite," whose meaning neither
observer nor observed can fathom. The speaker himself feels ghost-
like, disembodied; and the men, women and children he observes seem
themselves spectres of some imagined family of some distant and in-
definable past: "the windowed ones in their windowy world." Despite
the fact that the inhabitants of the house move

> As dead actors, on a rainy afternoon
> Move in a darkened living-room, for children
> Watching the world that was before they were,
>
> (232)

the speaker, "morose and speechless" in his narcissistic suffering of
"that time of troubles and of me," still wishes

> If only I were they!
> Could act out, in longing, the impossibility
> That haunts me like happiness!
>
> (232)

For the speaker, there is no getting outside the self. Without access to a fiction that might help him "cure that short disease, myself" (107), he watches life through a window like the children in the darkened living room on the other side of that window who stare into the television screen. The impossible wish for the speaker is to somehow join an idealized man and woman to create an imagined family, a creation he can never realize because he is afraid to articulate it (perhaps out of fear that nobody will listen to him). Even within his fantasy, attempts at communication with others meets silence, and his attempt to retreat to the security of, once again, the inadequate comforter, leaves him staring into a void:

> Some morning they will come downstairs and find me.
> They will start to speak, and then smile speechlessly,
> Shifting the plates, and set another place
> At a table by a silent fire.
> When I have eaten they will say, "You have not slept."
>
> And from the sofa, mounded in my quilt,
> My face on *their* pillow, that is always cool,
> I will look up speechlessly into a—
>
> (233)

As in "The Grown-Up," the world that the speaker perceives is "all image / And Imageless" (239), a world that is "silent, drowned in time" ("The Elementary Scene," 1935 version). The speechlessness in "Windows" with its heavy reliance on shadowy images, evokes a television world; one imagines the speaker passively looking into a screen suddenly gone dead with static, as the windows shut, and the family of *Father Knows Best* lives its secret life between episodes. Unable to escape the short disease of self, the speaker, too, waits to have his eyes closed by a hand that "moves so slowly that it does not move" (233).

"Windows" is decidedly a poem whose characters are reduced to surface perception and are unable to create or fabricate. In a poem published alongside "Windows" in *Poetry* (and in *The Woman at the Washington Zoo*), Jarrell explores further the difficulties of making "anything of anything" (234). As William Pritchard has observed, "Aging" is a kind of litmus, or "test case for separating those whose admiration for [Jarrell's] poetry is extreme, and those less enthusiastic" (134):

> I wake, but before I know it is done,
> The day, I sleep. And of days like these the years,
> A life is made. I nod, consenting to my life.
> . . . But who can live in these quick-passing hours?
> I need to find again, to make a life,
> A child's Sunday afternoon, the Pleasure Drive
> Where everything went by but time; the Study Hour
> Spent at a desk, with folded hands, in waiting.
>
> In those I could make. Did I not make in them
> Myself? The Grown One whose time shortens,
> Breath quickens, heart beats faster, till at last
> It catches, skips. . . . Yet those hours that seemed, were endless,
> Were still not long enough to have remade
> My childish heart: the heart that must have, always,
> To make anything of anything, not time,
> Not time but—
>   but, alas! eternity.
>
>   (234)

With Pritchard, I see Jarrell's nostalgia, "not as a debilitating limitation, an 'immaturity,' but as his special gift or curse, a unique way of making a life" (135). As "Aging" makes painfully clear, Jarrell uses nostalgia primarily to point out our debilitating limitations. As "Grown Ones," our time steadily shortening, we are granted one wish, "make me what I am" (257). In this century, the world has become a witch, like the witch in "Jamestown" that says to us,

> Mortal, because you have believed
> In your mortality, there is no wood, no wish,
> No world, there is only you. But what are you?
> The world has become you. But what are you?
>
> (257)

The man wastes his three wishes at Jamestown as modern adults have wasted theirs. Mastery over the world accelerates rather than suspends time: "From Jamestown, Virginia, to Washington, D.C., / Is, as the rocket flies, eleven minutes" (257).

In "Aging," and throughout this volume, Jarrell urgently asks "who can live in these quick-passing hours?" If life is, as Jarrell suggests, the ways we miss our lives, then our only recompense is far removed from the "Abundant recompense" of the high-Romantic vision in "Tintern Abbey." Though the world of childhood seems for the "aging" speaker the only place where one may rediscover and make a life, those "hours that seemed . . . endless / [are] still not long enough." As the character Irene Rosenbaum observes in *Pictures*, "nostalgia is the permanent condition of man" (162), but nostalgia does not restore to us the child's heart. Like Wordsworth, Jarrell is able only to "see by glimpses now"; childhood becomes merely "some fragment from his dream of human life." It seems that the inevitable awakening of adults to mortality undermines the confidence to "make" anything worthwhile or lasting. Childhood, a brief evanescence, cannot be remade for the adult; to make anything of anything, one needs immortality, eternity. But Jarrell, alas, as we all are, is "continually mortal," and he acts as a spokesman, "as next friend," to time-bound "aging machine-parts." Time shortening, the Grown One *needs* to recreate the "Sunday afternoon, the Pleasure Drive / . . . the Study Hour," but can only look back ruefully, helplessly. Nostalgia affirms the endless sense of the potentiality in childhood, but it also reminds the adult of how that wealth has been squandered. The speaker looks at Sunday, the Pleasure Drive, and the Study Hour and sees where they led: "Did I not make in them / Myself?"

What has happened? Beneath the nostalgia lurks an actual childhood. Though idealized by the Grown Ones, it was spent, as Jarrell makes clear throughout his work, "alone," beneath the inadequate comforter:

> And, yawning
> In my bed in my room, alone,
> I would look out: over the quilted
> Rooftops, the clear stars shone.
> How poor and miserable we were,
> How seldom together!
> And yet, after so long one thinks
> In those days everything was better.
> ("In Those Days," 1953, 230)

Nostalgia, Jarrell suggests, is our permanent, inadequate condition. We dream of connectedness, communication, speech; we dream a family that glorifies our childish wish for a perfect family, trying to forget that as children we were often poor and miserable and seldom together. Feeling that, given another chance, we could make a family, we are painfully aware of "the blind date that has stood [us] up: [our] life" (18). Looking back "after so long," and entertaining the possibility of the impossible offered in the wistful Jarrellian phrase "And yet . . . ," we find the embers of a more shameful recognition. How pitiful it is "to have one's life add up to *yet!*" (18). With the speaker of "The Player Piano" we might lament, "If only, somehow, I had learned to live!" (355), a cry answered by the Marschallin of "The Face":

> Here I am.
>   But it's not *right*.
> If living can do this,

Living is more dangerous than anything:
It is terrible to be alive.

(24)

That so many speakers in *The Woman at the Washington Zoo* are de-
scendants of the Marschallin underscores the widening gulf between
youth and age that Jarrell perceived and articulated in "Windows,"
"Aging," "In Those Days," and "The Elementary Scene" (revised version, 1960). In "The Elementary Scene" the speaker looks back on
his poor and miserable childhood and finds "a dead land waking sadly
to my life" (231). The misery of that dead land is apparent in the
imagery of childhood objects described as "rotten," "stinking," "cold,"
and "wooden." Though the child's world is miserable—the child is
"flushed" and "struggles into sleep"—the adult speaker's life is yet
more miserable; as he tries to revisit the child's world, the true horrors of the world that follows coalesce once again in the image of the
inadequate comforter:

Till leaning a lifetime to the comforter,
I float above the small limbs like their dream:
I, I, the future that mends everything.

(231)

Children have been reduced to limbs, as if torn apart; the adult speaker
has been reduced to a dream of those limbs. The last line is bitterly
ironic. The disembodied "I" floating above the limbs of the child cannot
mend anything.

It is impossible not to see in the futility of these lines a reflection
of the tenuousness of Jarrell's faith in the power of his own poetry to
transform, a diminution reflected in his inability to write new poems.
The translations in *The Woman at the Washington Zoo* are not merely
attempts to conquer this poetry-writing block, they are attempts to
make sense of the seemingly insurmountable gulf between child and

adult that lay at the heart of Jarrell's poetic silence.[1] So central are they to the volume, that the book could easily be subtitled with one of the Rilke translations, "Requiem for the Death of a Boy." The importance of the translations of Rilke's "Kindheit" and "Die Erwachsene" to Jarrell's image of childhood has already been explored in chapter 1, but "Requiem," written in 1915 after the beginning of the first World War, yields further insights into Jarrell's perception of what the twentieth century has meant to childhood. Jarrell's translation emphasizes the universality that Rilke intended in making the particular death of eight-year-old Peter Jaffe emblematic of the tragic devaluation of childhood in the modern world. Like "The Woman at the Washington Zoo," "Requiem" is a dramatic monologue, but it is spoken by a child from beyond the grave, not by an "aging machine-part." Where the woman at the zoo finds herself lost in the grown-up world of work and sex and money and death, the speaker of "Requiem" remembers feeling lost in a child's world that should have been reassuring to him, but was not. The boy has died "in the midst of play"; indeed, his play is a defense against the absences he perceives—the absence of family and the absence of God.

As in "The Orient Express," discussed in chapter 3, the child of "Requiem" experiences the outside world as "things from a primer":

> Why did I print upon myself the names
> Of Elephant and Dog and Cow
> So far off now, already so long ago,
> And Zebra too. . . . what for, what for?
> What holds me now
> Climbs like a water line
> Up past all that. What help was it to know
> I was, if I could never press
> Through what's soft, what's hard, and come at last
> Behind them, to the face that understands?

(247)

Living in a family without affection, the boy resorts to animistic thinking, finding only his toys "reliable." His impulse to rely on grown-ups
is constantly thwarted:

> Because that we all sat there together—
> I never did believe that. No honestly.
> You talked, you laughed, but none of you were ever
> Inside the talking or laughing. No.
>
> (248)

To fill the void, the child animates his playthings, a solution that proves
not only inadequate but dangerous. Trying to understand his loneliness
in terms of a wooden horse, the boy makes himself inanimate:

> Because almost from the start I understood
> How alone a wooden horse is. You can make one,
> A wooden horse, one any size,
> It gets painted, and later on you pull it,
> And it's the real street it pounds down, then.
> When you call it a horse, why isn't it a lie?
> Because you feel that you're a horse, a little,
> And grow all maney, shiny, grow four legs—
> So as to grow some day into a man?
> But wasn't I wood a little, too,
> For its sake, and grew hard and quiet
> And looked out at it from an emptier face?
>
> (248)

Little by little, to paraphrase the speaker of "The Lost Children"
(1965), the child in him dies: "I made myself at home with everything. /
Only everything was satisfied without me / And got sadder, hung about
with me" (249). Perhaps looking for his own face in other children, he
finds "They're always dying." Recognizing the difficulty of separation,
and his own inadequate understanding of the gulf between himself and
grown-ups, he laments that he "never got it right, exactly." He could

not make himself at home in the world because the world gets along in its usual way without him.

Of course the world also gets along without grown-ups. In the words of the woman at the zoo: "The world goes by my cage and never sees me." And what does the adult see? The death of childhood makes one look at the things of the world out of "an emptier face"; the grown-ups in Jarrell's translation of Rilke's "Das Kind," look at the child "Exhausted with their misery, enduring their lives, / They do not even see that he endures: / Endures everything" (254). That stoic endurance, however, even when extended into the afterlife, does not make God visible: "Here everyone is like a just-poured drink / But the ones who drink us I still haven't seen" (249).

Although many of Jarrell's characters experience living deaths, Jarrell wishes to make us aware through art that life and death are not the same, even though they may sometimes seem or "sound the same" (328). Jarrell explores the ramifications of life without God by updating the riddle of the sphinx. In "The Sphinx's Riddle to Oedipus" (1953) the riddle of the sphinx is transformed into one whose answer is not "man" but "the sphinx," as if the only way to answer the riddle of life is with the riddle itself: "what has a woman's breasts, a lion's paws?" Without divine authority, any answer is ultimately meaningless, and the inevitable response to that void is blindness: "not to have guessed is better" because "to understand / Is to pluck out one's own eyes with one's own hands" (270). Understanding oneself exacts too high a price. Oedipus's ironic blindness is that he can see others' condition but not his own; the modern dilemma is articulated in the answer to the question posed by the last poem in *The Complete Poems,* "What's The Riddle?" (1965): "I don't know," again repeated three times in the poem. In the twentieth century, the meaningful trinity has been replaced by the tripartite denial that is characteristic in Jarrell's poetry.

The tripartite denial, of course, also echoes Peter's three denials of Christ. In Jarrell's criticism of Elizabeth Bishop's "Roosters" (which he called one of "the most calmly beautiful, deeply sympathetic poems of our time"), Jarrell notes the "inescapable hope," even in the face of the denials, that makes Bishop's work "morally so attractive":

> Instead of crying, with justice, "This is a world in which no one can get along," Miss Bishop's poems show that it is barely but perfectly possible —has been, that is, for her. Her work is unusually personal and honest in its wit, perception, and sensitivity—and in its restrictions too; all her poems have written underneath *I have seen it.* She is morally so attractive, in poems like "The Fish" or "Roosters," because she understands so well that the wickedness and confusion of the age can explain and extenuate other people's wickedness and confusion, but not, for you, your own; that morality, for the individual, is usually a small, personal, statistical, but heartbreaking or heart-warming affair of omissions and commissions the greatest of which will seem infinitesimal, ludicrously beneath notice, to those who govern, rationalize, and deplore; that it is sometimes difficult and unnatural, but sometimes easy and natural to "do well"; that beneath our lives "there is inescapable hope, the pivot," so that in the revolution of things even the heartsick Peter can someday find "his dreadful rooster come to mean forgiveness." (*Poetry and the Age* 234–35)

Like Bishop, Jarrell wants to believe in the "necessary Ideal just beyond the fringes of the terrible Actual" (Chappell 23), and he tries to posit the lost world of childhood and the potential lost world of art as replacements for the absent deity. He has faith in "inescapable hope, the pivot" that might be found in those lost worlds, but the poems in *The Woman at the Washington Zoo* show how ephemeral those worlds may be. Uncritical faith in them can be as misleading and self-wounding as following the Mockingbird's song will prove to be in *The Bat-Poet,* explored in the next chapter.

Humanity tries to tap the resources of the lost worlds, but finds that they provide only a "momentary stay against confusion." Art in the real world has fallen prey to the confusion we suffer in the twentieth century. As the essay "The End of the Line" (1942) makes explicit, Jarrell believes that society's betrayal of the child culminates in the chaos signified by modern warfare, and that this sound and fury finds itself mirrored in the artistic dead end of modernism. Modern art has abandoned the effort to join the fragments of human experience in order to remake meaning, and has settled for mere representation of that fragmentation. That abdication further blurs the distinctions between childhood and maturity, leaving us adolescently split between the two worlds. In a supreme irony, abstract art, waving its banner of nonrepresentation (which Jarrell lampooned in "The Age of the Chimpanzee," retitled "Against Abstract Expressionism" in *Kipling, Auden, and Co.*), threatens to be finally representational, depicting the earth as a mere "planet among galaxies":

> Christ disappears, the dogs disappear: in abstract
> Understanding, without admiration, the last master puts
> Colors on canvas, a picture of the universe
> In which a bright spot somewhere in the corner
> Is the small radioactive planet men called Earth.
>
> (333)

When art is victimized by the age and abandons its higher calling, it not only loses its power to transform but salts the earth from which transformation springs. Myths become debased, as in Jarrell's terrifying vision of Sleeping Beauty cruelly murdered in "La Belle au Bois Dormant" or in his "Cinderella" diminished into "a sullen wife and a reluctant mother" silenced by the fires of Hell. The secularization of the sacred has turned Jarrell's St. Jerome inside out. He is the psychiatrist whose lion is encaged in a zoo. The possibility of adoration has vanished under the light of reason. Values, no longer rooted in belief, become ghostly. And as the spiritual dissolves, Jerome's development (and ours) reverses course—in his dream, Id replaces Ego; and human history is not the story of life's progression but its march toward self-destruction.

Describing his life during the first World War, Rilke remarked: "During almost all the War-years I was . . . waiting in Munich, always thinking it MUST come to an end, not understanding, not understanding, not understanding! NOT TO UNDERSTAND: yes, that was my whole occupation during those years" (Leishman 11). Prefiguring the tripartite "I don't know's" of Jarrell's poetry, Rilke recognized that his self-numbing reaction to the horrors of modern warfare was suffused with guilt. In the same way, the refusal to understand one's condition is the source of oceanic guilt and dread in Jarrell's poetry. Articulation of denial is one of the uses of art, and *The Woman at the Washington Zoo* offers a kind of qualified faith, "inescapable hope, the pivot." But it is a faith so qualified that it sometimes seems a poor faith indeed. Jarrell argues for a remembrance, born out of our acknowledgment of denial, that will make action possible, and break the spell that paralyzes us. He argues that to enter the kingdom of art we must become as little children, must try to reenter a world where we can "make." True art not only accuses us, but insists, "You must change your life."

Jarrell explores the alternative futures of art through two artists in this volume—one a major figure, the other minor. In "The End of the Rainbow" the focus is on the persona of the artist; in "The Bronze David of Donatello" the focus is on the work of art. In "Rainbow," the minor artist, Content, revels in her unawareness, her artiness, but is haunted by what she has not made. In the second poem, the person of Donatello vanishes into the bronze David he has cast, a creation emblematic of the dawning Renaissance concept of self-awareness. It is a creation so potent, according to Jarrell, that its expression of fundamental truth about humanity transcends the society in which it was created and speaks to us in ways the artist did not foresee.

Content, in "The End of the Rainbow," is a grown-up who has not, in fact, grown up, but is an arrested adolescent. Alone with her mocking artifacts, she feels entirely displaced, living in the fool's gold at the wrong end of the rainbow in California—a place so divorced from tradition that when people send letters to the East they drop them in a mailbox marked "THE STATES." Content is a "near relation" of figures like the woman at the zoo and the girl in the library—her life adds up to "and yet." She is an even closer relative of the speaker of "The

Player Piano" (1965), since her continual lament seems to be, "If only somehow I had learned to live!" Like the woman in "Next Day" (1963) she repeats to herself, "I'm old," and like the Marschallin of "The Face" (1950), she feels "It is terrible to be alive." She is not deluded into thinking her art is successful; her art mirrors her failed life. She is like both Jarrell's "Cinderella" and Snow White's stepmother:

> She murmurs as she used to murmur: "Men!"

> She looks into the mirror and says: "Mirror,
> Who is the fairest of us all?

> According to the mirror, it's the mirror.
>   (225)

The valuable myths of Content's childhood—*Water Babies*, "The Frog Prince," *Little Women* and *Little Men*, "The Little Mermaid," *Swiss Family Robinson*, and others—have been superseded by homilies. She reads Mary Baker Eddy, Emerson's *Compensation*, and cherishes the same debased cliches as the father in "The Night Before the Night Before Christmas": "HE WHO HAS HIMSELF FOR A FRIEND IS BEST BEFRIENDED—this in gothic" (225). She is, in short, hopelessly content with her discontent, with living a manless, childless, fleshless existence:

> She says: "Look at my life. Should I go on with it?
> It seems to you I have . . . a real gift?
> I shouldn't like to keep on if I only. . . .
> It seems to you my life is a success?
> Death answers, *Yes. Well, yes.*
>   (228)

But the telltale quilt mirrors the truth about her colorless life, her patchwork art:

> How many colors, squeezed from how many tubes
> In patient iteration, have made up the world

She draws closer, like a patchwork quilt,
To warm her all the long, summer day!
She hangs here on the verge of seeing
In black and white,
And turns with an accustomed gesture
To the easel saying:
"Without my paintings I would be—

why, whatever *would I be?"*
(228)

Her arty kitsch has kept Content content in a way, but at a price. In order for her to remain pacified, she must erase herself, must obliterate the disappointments and the joys of her youth, and forget both the myths and the sad realities of her life:

Safe from all nightmares
One comes upon awake in the world, she sleeps.
She sleeps in sunlight, surrounded by many dreams
Or dreams of dreams, all good—how can a dream be bad
If it keeps one asleep?

(228)

Content, in short, ignores the uneasiness of active dreaming; she has a glimmer of awareness about her dissatisfaction but prefers to remain unaware of its origins or implications, projecting her all-too-human wish for "good" dreams upon her dog Su-Su IV, who "can dream / His own old dream: that he is sleeping." Looking at the inadequacy of both her art and life, she tries not to see, basking in a waking sleep of her own miscreation.

"The Bronze David of Donatello" is a telling counterpoint to "The End of the Rainbow" that underscores the underlying theme of the volume—the lament for lost childhood embodied in Rilke's "Requiem for the Death of a Boy." The Bronze David was the first large freestanding nude since antiquity, and is often cited by art historians as a paradigm for the Renaissance theme of self-recognition. Donatello's David does, indeed, appear to be regarding himself rather than the severed head of Goliath.² In Jarrell's eyes, this David seems inhuman: naked yet clothed; sexless, yet with "a face that holds us like the whore Medusa's" (273). Drawn to this self-regarding face, the face that has succumbed entirely to "that short disease myself," we are turned to stone. As in Rilke's "Kindheit," recognition of self leads to loss of self. David is shameless and complacent, exalted out of all proportion— "Angelic, almost, in indifference." It is a self-involvement so final as to be severed from the rest of humanity, to be essentially inhuman:

> Centering itself upon itself, the sleek
> Body with its too-large head, this green
> Fruit now forever green, this offending
> And efficient elegance draws subtly, supply
> Between the world and itself, a shining
> Line of delimitation, demarcation.
>
> (273–74)

Awakening to self-regard by his victory over Goliath, David has been cast, in bronze, from the world. Frozen, like Medusa gazing into Perseus's shield, he reminds one of Wallace Stevens's Snow Man, one who, though living, "must have been cold a long time" to be so cut off from "the sound of misery." David has become "nothing himself" through his self-appraising detachment, "And nothing himself, beholds / Nothing that is not there and the nothing that is" (Stevens 10). He becomes a frozen metaphor of an icy inhuman existence.

This David bears a marked resemblance to the monstrous child in Jarrell's later poem "The One Who Was Different," and the speakers of both poems eventually turn their attentions—in "David's" case, to the corpse of Goliath—in order to lead us toward something human. For Jarrell, the major accomplishment of real artists like Donatello is to help us identify with the human, with "something that there's something wrong with." The function of art is to help us live life, not escape it. The speaker's attention shifts our attention from the frozen, indifferent, inhuman David to the severed head of the human, fallen, blessed Goliath, ironically deflating the false heroism of our age by implying that to identify oneself with humanity has become philistine. The figure of David has become timeless, eternal, David himself has not. Deluded by his victory, he does not see how he shares the fate of the vanquished. The reader, viewer, and speaker, however, know that, "alas, eternity" does not exist for time-bound Grown Ones: to be human is to accept, unwillingly, blessed defeat. David "looks down at the head and does not see it":

> Upon his head
> As upon a spire, the boy David dances,
> Dances, and is exalted.
> > Blessed are those brought low,
> Blessed is defeat, sleep blessed, blessed death.
>
> > > (275)

This is Jarrell's own, humanized Sermon on the Mount—and the last words in the volume. Christ has become "just man," and though we try to recapture divinity through lost childhood or art, as in "Nestus Gurley," we always fall short. The best we can do is to look upon our fellow mortal creatures with sympathy and empathy. The great work of art, then, ironically affirms our limitations rather than our ambitions. Yet in revealing the "unknown, unwanted life" at the heart of our limitation, we can be spurred into a true quest for ourselves.

To do otherwise is to succumb to the "great big moral vacuum" Jarrell detected "at the heart of E. E. Cummings's poetry (*Kipling, Auden* 168). Great art is as unforgiving of smug idolatry as Jarrell was of Cummings, whose poems he thought as morally disastrous as he thought Bishop's morally attractive. In a review attacking Cummings's palatable and decadent version of modernism, Jarrell admonishes the reader with his definition of great art, an art he saw embodied in one of the greatest poems by his beloved Rilke:

Rilke, in his wonderful "Archaic Statue of Apollo," ends his description of the statue, the poem itself, by saying without transition or explanation:

You must change your life. He needs no explanation. We know from many
experiences that this is what the work of art does: its life—in which we
have shared the alien existences both of this world and of that different
world to which the work of art alone gives us access—unwillingly accuses
our lives. (*Kipling, Auden* 166)

If we are to "make anything of anything," we must connect ourselves
with the world and capture a small eternity; we are truly doomed when
we feel "that we and the poet are so superior to the fools and ped-
ants and reformers of the world that our only obligation is to condemn
them" (*Kipling, Auden* 167).

Jarrell's praise of Bishop, that "all her poems have written underneath '*I have seen it*,'" was high praise indeed from the critic whose
favorite line from Whitman was, "I am the man, I suffered, I was
there." Jarrell comments:

In the last lines of this quotation Whitman has reached—as great writers
always reach—a point at which criticism seems not only unnecessary but
absurd: these lines are so good that even admiration feels like insolence,
and one is ashamed of anything one can find to say about them. How
anyone can dismiss or accept patronizingly the man who wrote them, I
do not understand. (*Poetry and the Age* 127)

Jarrell in his criticism regularly appeals to and for informed Taste.
Yet his appeal goes further by treating ordinary gut feelings as being
worthy of attention, a prelude to finding our moral bedrock, a fusion of
art and life. He advocates, finally, a maturity which hears the world's
anguished, expectant whisper: "*Here I am*."

SIX

Happy Families Are
All Invented

In early 1962, according to Mary Jarrell's commentary in *Randall
Jarrell's Letters*, while he was hospitalized for hepatitis, Jarrell

> received a letter from Michael di Capua, a junior editor in children's
> books at Macmillan who knew his poetry. From reading "The Märchen,"
> di Capua had gotten the idea of asking Jarrell to choose and translate
> some of Grimm's tales for a series of children's books that included trans-
> lations by writers such as Jean Stafford for "Arabian Nights" and Isak
> Dinesen for Hans Christian Andersen. Jarrell thought this quite imagi-
> native, "especially using Jean for the 'Arabian Nights,'" and he picked
> "Snow White" and "The Fisherman's Wife" [*sic*] to translate and began
> to improve. (453–54)

Later that spring, she relates, di Capua encouraged Jarrell to write an
original children's book:

> just as he had associated "The Märchen" with Grimm's tales, he saw in
> Jarrell's children's poems the possibility of a children's story. Intrigued
> again, Jarrell stationed himself outdoors in a hammock under the pines,
> among the cardinals and chipmunks, and, with the stereo volume turned
> up, wrote *The Gingerbread Rabbit* and started on *The Bat-Poet*. (455)

Jarrell's interest in writing for children lent a new vitality to all his
writing, but also served to reinforce his apprehensiveness about aging.

To Robert Lowell he wrote, "I feel pretty young myself but I admit there're two houses near whose children call, 'Santa Claus! Hi Santa Claus!'" (457). To Robert Penn Warren he wrote, "I translated some German fairy tales for a nice children's editor, Michael di Capua, and before I knew it I'd written a children's book too. Now I've written half of another. It feels queer and entertaining to write the sort of thing you've never written before" (460). Jarrell's writing for children and his association with di Capua proved to be more than merely "queer and entertaining." He approached all of his writing for the next year and a half with manic intensity, finishing his translations of *The Three Sisters* and *Faust, Part 1*, half of the poems for *The Lost World*, four children's books, and beginning work on an anthology of modern poetry. The ideal audience for children's books, Jarrell was to say many times in interviews and letters, was not exclusively an audience of children. Rather, he liked to think of his stories as "half for children, half for grown-ups" (Mary Jarrell "Liner Notes").

Similarly, Jarrell's perception of the poet as someone who is a "once a child" (in the phrase from his translation of Rilke's "The Grown-Up" [239]) sheds light on the children's books. Children, Jarrell believed, have already the spirit of a poet, though they cannot articulate this spirit in poetry. For Jarrell, as for Wordsworth in *The Prelude*,[1] the success of the adult poet is contingent on his or her ability to retain or recapture the poetic spirit of childhood and to articulate it. Without recourse to that spirit, the poet is unable to create poetry as distinguished from mere "verse." Echoing the scriptures, Jarrell says in *A Sad Heart at the Supermarket*, "unless ye be converted and become as little children, ye shall not enter into the kingdom of art" (95). To be sure, Jarrell insists not that one should become a child, but rather that one should become "as a child," retaining contact with the childhood that was "once." Like Wordsworth, Jarrell sees poetry as a dialogue between the primary, nature-connected spirit of childhood and the mature, expressive powers of humanity. Though the "lost world" of childhood and the world of maturity conflict, the aim of the poet is not to escape from the adult world into the "lost world," like Peter Pan, but to transform the world of maturity imaginatively.

Jarrell rebels against the Edwardian cult of the child as innocent. His vision of childhood includes Wordsworthian "fear," and the violence of the Brothers Grimm and Rilke: children's lives are "full of sorcerers and ogres" (106), images of darkness that equal those of adult fantasy. His training in psychology led him to observe the darker aspects of a child's animism in a 1935 letter to Robert Penn Warren:

> I've had to interrupt this letter for an hour to play with a three-year-old boy that visited us. He was very interesting telling about the dark man, and the rain man, and the thunder man. They live above the clouds, in the sky, with God; God makes them do what they do. The dark man is all covered with dark, the thunderman with thunder. The dark man doesn't live in the sun, but along with the rest of them. He got me to draw him a picture of the dark man. The dark man looks exactly the same as he does, except he is grown up. At night after he goes to sleep he thinks about the dark man; he doesn't play in his dreams or do anything except think about the dark man. (3)

The natural world is not innocent but "charged" by the child's dreams of a hidden self. Similarly, the family is not only a natural but also an imaginative construct, perhaps the first instance of the child's poetic activity.

Becoming as a child or "once a child" is virtually a religious task; it involves transcending mere childlikeness. To be a poet of childhood does not mean to speak as a child; it means to put away childish things, but not to forget them. Jarrell makes this connection in a letter to Sister Bernetta Quinn in 1951: "I know I am childlike in one sense (since I can do handwriting analysis, I can see it in my writing) and I'd like to be in the other, more important sense, that of the Gospels" (*Letters* 304).

The Gingerbread Rabbit (1964) introduces the major theme of Jarrell's fiction for children, not surprisingly also the theme of *Pictures from an Institution,* the need for happy yet improbable families that do not exist in the real world but have to be invented. Indeed, Jarrell's preoccupation with the relationship between the child and a natural or created family became an obsession in his later work, and nowhere is this obsession more pronounced than in his writing for children. In the past, critics of Jarrell's children's books have tended to stress the theme of the child's estrangement from and nostalgia for the family. Maurice Sendak, for example, has observed, "I know how desperately Randall needed a family. That's the whole message of everything he wrote—this incredible *need* for a family" (Griswold, *Children's Books* 112). The topic is most fully developed in Jerome Griswold's interpretation of the children's books in light of "separation anxiety." In Griswold's view, the master plot of these stories is the male child's quest to regain his mother's affection, an Oedipal quest.[2] Among the other critics who touch briefly on this topic, Leo Zanderer traces in three of these books the child as "explorer or seeker" whose heroic journey helps the reader overcome "the image of man fatally anchored to his role in society" (78). And John Updike, who lists Jarrell's "habitual themes of individual lostness, of estrangement within a family, of the magic of language, of the wild beauty beyond our habitations," notes briefly but tellingly, "Jarrell's vision of bliss [is] adoption by members of another species" (59).

In contrast to the regressive movement Griswold observes, Updike's comments suggest a creative, outward bound quest for family. Yet that substitute family is not the adult, sexual relationship one might expect. As Roger Sale points out in *Fairy Tales and After,* Jarrell wishes to write about a mythical family in which familial affection is separate from sexual affection (88).

One of the reasons that the theme of family acquired such resonance in Jarrell's oeuvre is that he fused his theory of child development with a theory of poetic development. His preoccupation with childhood found significant expression not only in his decision to experiment with children as an audience but in his theory of poetic voice. Significantly, both his theory of the audience and of the poet stress a "composite entity" of the adult and the child.

Jarrell found his way to the full expression of these themes gradually, at first adopting other writers' plots as they seemed to fit his needs, then elaborating his own. The plot of *The Gingerbread Rabbit,* Jarrell's first original book for children following his translations of the tales of Grimm and Ludwig Bechstein, is a curious amalgam of the plots of the traditional tale "The Gingerbread Man" and Margery Williams's *The Velveteen Rabbit.* Even Garth Williams's illustrations recall those of William Nicholson in *The Velveteen Rabbit.* The sentimental theme of Jarrell's story is the same as that of *The Velveteen Rabbit:* an imaginary animal, a rabbit, escapes destruction by an adult, and by being loved, becomes "real." In *The Gingerbread Rabbit,* a mother makes a gingerbread rabbit for her daughter to replace a real rabbit that has run away into the forest. In the midst of her baking, she is distracted by a vegetable man, and the gingerbread rabbit comes to life, runs away, is deceived and nearly eaten by a fox, but escapes with a real rabbit who takes him home to his wife and adopts him.

Jarrell's own unstable family may be reflected in the human family of *The Gingerbread Rabbit,* which consists of a mother and her only child, Mary, who live in lonely isolation on the edge of the forest. Though Mary's father is mentioned in the book, he is conspicuously absent from the story, just as Jarrell's father was absent in his youth. The mother in the story seems a "near relation" of the speaker of "Next Day." She is nervous, harried, and lonely—a characterization reinforced by Garth Williams's illustrations. This mother is always having to make the best of bad situations; she is forced to accept substitutes as a matter of course, and the rabbit himself is a substitute for the real rabbit that will not be there when her daughter gets home from school. From our adult perspective the mother seems, above all, "distracted." Indeed, it is when she is distracted by the vegetable man that the gingerbread protagonist comes to life. From the gingerbread rabbit's perspective we see the mother's latent violence: in a comical conversation with a paring knife, a mixing bowl, and a rolling pin, he discovers that his fate is to be cooked and eaten. He has no feeling for his sad creator, whom he sees as a pursuing giant.

The gingerbread rabbit is a true innocent, and as such he is much less interesting than the later protagonists; he seems to possess the child's ignorance and gullibility without any serious indication of the child's potential. The real loss experienced by the child Mary finds no expression. Furthermore, the evocation of family values in the rabbit warren after the gingerbread rabbit has been adopted seems reductively materialistic: "carrots and watercress," "this nice rushy bed," and "hide-and-seek" (42–43). Emotional ties and needs remain undeveloped, as do the risks of pain involved in human relationships. In contrast with later created families, the rabbit family into which the gingerbread rabbit stumbles seems not only fictional, but unbelievable.

And yet, adoption is the heart of the matter for Jarrell. Commenting to Michael di Capua, Jarrell expresses his pleasure with the illustrations by Garth Williams: "The old rabbit in the colored sketch makes me want to be adopted by him" (*Letters* 464). As one of the notes in the manuscript of *The Gingerbread Rabbit* stresses: "FAMILY ROMANCE // parents not real parents." In the gingerbread rabbit's quest for freedom we may see an embodiment of the Freudian "family romance," whose expression Jarrell so admired in Kipling (*Sad Heart* 137). Significantly, Freud theorizes that the child comes to terms with the apparent hostility of the parents by splitting them into good and evil pairs, a pattern we see here in the opposed human and animal families of Jarrell's gingerbread child. Even more important, the child copes with evident signs of parental weakness by fantasies about "true" parents. In fantasy, the child invents a story of adoption, seeking "the replacement of both parents or of the father alone by grander people . . . equipped with attributes that are derived entirely from real recollections of the actual and humble ones" ("Family Romances" 9:240).

One of Freud's remarks that must have been seminal for Jarrell was his observation that this "romancing," normal among children, may continue for certain adults: "a quite peculiarly marked imaginative activity is one of the essential characteristics of neurotics and also of all comparatively gifted people" (9:240). Jarrell takes this point further, metaphorically tying the adoption fantasies of the child to the imaginative activity of the artist. Families are works of art just as poems are, and because they are works of art, they can be successfully created only by someone who retains the Rilkean sense of being "once a child"—the mature artist drawing on the poetic spirit of childhood and articulating it.

If *The Gingerbread Rabbit* through its inherited narrative structure lays stress on flight from the threatening parent (since the rabbit family is discovered only by accident), *Fly by Night* (1976) stresses the quest, the lonely child's turn to fantasy to invent a family.[3] These two books represent two poles in Jarrell's central theme. On the one hand, the child attempts to seek definition as an individual—"a single, separate being"; on the other, he or she seeks to become a member of a community or "plural being," a family.

The protagonist of *Fly by Night,* David, seems very close to the speaker of Jarrell's best poems about lonely children such as "A Sick Child," "A Story," or "The Elementary Scene." David also resembles the Jarrell of "The Lost World," when he grieves to leave his tree house for reality: "He sits in it so much that the sparrows are used to him, and light just out of reach in the branches" (4). Also like Jarrell, David's playmates are animals—"there aren't any children for him to play with" (4). He has an occasional conversation with the mailman, reminiscent of "A Sick Child," but for the most part his daytime existence is mundane and very lonely. But "at night David can fly" (4).

David's flight takes him through the house where he sees his parents' dreams without really understanding them, and through the night, where he sees the disturbing dreams of his pets, who dream of their prey.[4] As he continues his journey, different animals such as sheep and ponies elude him, until at last an owl invites him to become "An owl till morning" (18). David watches the owl feed her owlets in a scene reminiscent of the cardinal scene in *The Bat-Poet,* and finally hears her tell them "The Owl's Bedtime Story." "The Owl's Bedtime Story" (written in terza rima like "The Lost World") both reassures David about the value of familial affection, and reminds him of what he lacks —the company of other children.

As always, Jarrell's fictional world is populated with only children and incomplete families. The owlet has a sister and at the end of the bedtime story, the mother and both her children nestle together, but the children have no father. David sees how affectionate they are, despite their father's absence, and it helps him come to terms with his own family, without siblings and distanced from his father. David's subconscious both removes his father, who has removed himself from David's lonely daytime world, and gives him the siblings he longs to have.

Ultimately, *Fly by Night* may disconcert by its apparent pessimism, for it does not resolve David's daytime problems. David wakes up, and as usual, he forgets his dream; he is able only to fly by night. The dream world is ambiguous. Is it a retreat? Or as the site of dream-work, does it suggest the function of imaginative retelling and the child's own quest to realize new values?

As *Fly by Night* shows, there is a nocturnal side to the child's quest, the darker aspect of the romance Jarrell noticed in Freud, in the märchen, and in Kipling: "The world [is] a dark forest full of families: so that when your father and mother leave you in the forest to die, the wolves that come to eat you are always Father Wolf and Mother Wolf, your real father and real mother, and you are—as not even the little wolves ever quite are—their real son" (*Sad Heart* 137). Kipling's identification of the adoptive family with wild animals clearly touched Jarrell's imagination. Autonomy and abandonment, adoption and devouring envelopment define the quandary of the child.

A family cannot become a true one until it is affirmed by choice—the sense Jarrell's boy protagonists must gain is not only that they are wanted, but that their own choices matter too. Both poets and children, these boys want to have it both ways—they want to be original and highly individual while at the same time they want to be accepted by society. But their quest for acceptance by society in real life is doomed; as Jarrell notes in "Poets, Critics and Readers," "The public has an unusual relationship to the poet; it doesn't even know he is there" (*Sad Heart* 90).

It is this difficult task of creating a chosen relationship, of establishing a poetic family, that shapes the narrative of *The Bat-Poet* (1964) and *The Animal Family* (1965). The bat-poet is an extraordinarily talented prodigy—one of the "Children who are different" (MS of "Childhood," UNC, Greensboro). His quest is both a child's quest and Jarrell's quest, in that it combines a need for an understanding family with that for an accepting audience. The end of the story hints at success but remains ambiguous; the public says to the unique lyrics of the poet what the bats say to the bat-poet: "When you say things like that, we don't know what you mean."

Like the unique artist, the bat-poet differs from the other bats: "a little bright brown bat, the color of coffee with cream in it" (1). Because he is a poet, he is estranged from a society he longs desperately to be a part of; he wants above all to say his poems to the other bats, but they are unwilling to listen to him. Like Jarrell, the bat-poet sees that society has "taken away his audience," and he seeks out the audiences of poets of other species (The Mockingbird) and of naifs (the Chipmunk); but, in truth, the only audience that the bat cares deeply about is the audience of his fellow bats. When he finds an attentive audience in the chipmunk, the bat mimics the mockingbird by saying, "It's a pleasure to say a poem to—to such a responsive audience" (17–18), yet he mimics not only the mockingbird's words, but his insincerity as well. For the bat wants more than a superficially "responsive" audience; he wants an audience that will be truly appreciative of his poems —in short, a community or family. Poetry, to the bat, is an exchange like the purest kind of chosen familial affection.

In *The Bat-Poet,* the development of the poet echoes the development of a child. When the other bats move into the barn, away from the comfortable home of the porch rafters, he wants them to come back, but somehow feels that he cannot join them in the barn. Like a child growing up he has a sense of being separate from the family and a sense that he is powerless to remedy this; able to become an artist only because he is an outcast, he still has a profound desire to be a part of the group if he can do it without sacrificing his autonomy. So he begins to be a poet by adopting a mentor, and by imitation. The transformation from imitator to creator involves a crisis of self-recognition similar to those described in Rilke's "The Grown-up" and "Childhood."

The uneasiness that the bat feels when he tries to write about the cardinal might well be attributed to the repressed memories of his own childhood. He notices that the cardinal feeds his children even though they're old enough to feed themselves[5]; the bat is not fully conscious of the loss of his own family, but it disturbs him so much that he cannot write about the cardinal. This intimation of his need for family combined with his growing dissatisfaction with imitation keeps the bat from writing another vivid but superficial "portrait in verse" like "The Chipmunk's Day."[6] Instead, the bat needs to escape the influence of his mentor, the mockingbird.

In "The Mockingbird," the bat recognizes that the mockingbird's song, though it is a convincing imitation of life, is not life itself. The bat admires the mockingbird, who is unquestionably a real poet and a mentor, as Tate and Ransom were to Jarrell, but he comes to see that his art is mostly artifice and his criticism pedantic. The mockingbird imitates what he drives away: he is more interested in imitation than in life. He may be able to imitate the world "so well" that one can't tell "Which one's the mockingbird? Which one's the world?" but it is only "for a moment, in the moonlight." Rather than imitate a world he drives away, the bat-poet wants to make poems that will reconcile him with the world, particularly with the world of the other bats who will re-constitute his family.

By becoming a poet, the bat overcomes his wish to remain a child at all costs, but he does not forget his childhood; rather he taps its poetic resources and through the mature, articulate means of the adult artist, transforms them into poetry. With the creation of his last and best poem he finally becomes a "once a child"—an adult who is able to use successfully the promise of childhood, not with a false nostalgia, but with an ability to remember its true nature. The poem "Bats" when it comes, comes easily: "all he had to do was remember what it had been like and every once in a while put in a rhyme"(35). First, he is able to write a poem that the other bats will be able to understand, and second, he finds his own style as a poet. The poem marks his emergence from his apprenticeship.

By remembering "what it is like to be a child," without reverting to infancy, the bat-poet is able to rejoin the others, to snuggle closer to them as the mother "folds her wings about her sleeping child." Becoming a "once a child," the bat-poet successfully becomes both a poet and an adult. He is able to leave his childhood home, confront the loss of his mother and father, and join his new family. It is significant that Jarrell ends *The Bat-Poet* ambiguously. The bat-poet does not get to say his poem to the other bats, which indicates the vanishing and fragile nature of the fictional family; it is important that the bat-poet adopt the family of bats on faith, a faith that transforms a vanishing fiction into a sustaining one.

Like *The Bat-Poet, The Animal Family* is about making a family as a poet makes a poem. But the major difference between *The Animal Family* and Jarrell's other children's fiction is that it does not have a child or childlike protagonist. Furthermore, *The Animal Family* transcends its precursor text, as the weaker books do not. Roger Sale has pointed out that Jarrell's family romance is influenced by Hans Christian Andersen's "The Little Mermaid," and Jarrell's familiarity with Andersen's story is clear from the poem "A Soul":

It is evening. One bat dances
Alone, where there were swallows.
The waterlilies are shadowed
With cattails, the cattails with willows.

The moon sets; after a little
The reeds sigh from the shore.
Then silence. There is a whisper,
"Thou art here once more."

In the castle someone is singing.
"Thou art warm and dry as the sun."
You whisper, and laugh with joy.
"Yes, here is one,

"Here is the other . . . *Legs* . . .
And they move so?"
I stroke the scales of your breast, and answer:
"Yes, as you know."

But you murmur, "How many years
Thou hast wandered there above!
Many times I had thought thee lost
Forever, my poor love.

"How many years, how many years
Thou hast wandered in air, thin air!
Many times I had thought thee lost,
My poor soul, forever."

(73)

In *The Animal Family,* the hunter shares the Bat-Poet's feeling that "the trouble isn't making poems, the trouble's finding somebody that will listen to them." The hunter is in harmony with nature, but he is also alone with nature. His land is a magical and beautiful one, but he has no one to share it with:

> In spring the meadow that ran down from the cliff to the beach was all foam-white and sea-blue with flowers; the hunter looked at it and it was beautiful. But when he came home there was no one to tell what he had seen—and if he picked the flowers and brought them home in his hands there was no one to give them to. And when at evening, past the dark blue shape of a far-off island, the sun sank under the edge of the sea like a red world vanishing, the hunter saw it all, but there was no one to tell what he had seen. (8)

It is apparent from the beginning that the hunter lacks more than an audience; what he misses, what makes his loneliness profound, is a family—not just a mother, as has been suggested, but a complete family consisting of father and mother and child. In his dreams, the hunter remembers his lost family. He lies in his bed listening

> to the great soft sound the waves made over and over. It seemed to him that it was like his mother singing. And before he could remember that his father and mother were dead and that he lived there all alone, he had drifted off to sleep—and in his sleep his mother sat by the bed singing, and his father sat at the fireplace waxing his bowstring or mending his long white arrows. (7–8)

One senses, reading this passage, the same nostalgia Jarrell evokes in "Children's Arms"; the hunter's father reminds one of "Pop" who helps the young Jarrell fashion "The bow that only Odysseus can wield." The hunter longs for an end to his isolation, for companionship, and for the security of domestic routine—the "ways that habit itself makes holy," but, of course, his parents are dead, the past is only a dream. Drawn by the sound of the sea that reminds him of his mother, he courts and wins a mermaid who, unable to accept the sea-people's dictum that "all good comes from the sea," is attracted to the land because "the land is new." If the land is new to the mermaid, the mermaid is new to the hunter, and together they begin to invent a family.

Like Jarrell, the hunter has an intense need for a family. After he and the mermaid have "lived together a long time," this need pervades his dreams. His earlier, wistful dream of domestic security is transformed into a nightmare of a broken, incomplete family, a shadow of a family because it is childless. The hunter has lost his childhood because he has lost his parents, and, because he is not a parent himself, the loss of childhood amounts to a loss of self:

> "My father was standing by the fire and he was double, like a man and his shadow—I was his shadow. And my mother sat there singing, and she was double too, like a woman and her shadow; and when I looked at it you were her shadow. But when I looked over to where I used to lie on the floor by the fire, there was nothing, not even a shadow; the place was empty. And the empty place got dark, and the fire went out, and I woke." (59–60)

"It's a bad dream," the mermaid says, though she knows it is a dream the hunter can't help dreaming, and she proceeds to interpret the dream as the hunter's wish for a child.

But, since there are "no human beings from whom they could beg or borrow or steal a child," they experiment, like the bat-poet, and adopt animal children. First they take in a bear whose mother the hunter has killed, and then a lynx who is stolen from his mother. Though they are quite fond of their animal children, the hunter and the mermaid quickly recognize that the bear and the lynx are not really "boys": The lynx grows to be unmanageable and is unavoidably feline, and they observe that having a bear who sleeps all winter is like having "Sleeping Beauty for a pet" (85). Finally a boy, the only child who is not ill-gotten, is washed ashore in the arms of his dead mother. In fact, the hunter is not the agent of the boy's joining the family at all; the boy is discovered by the lynx and brought back by the lynx and the bear. But it is clear from the moment of the boy's arrival that he is much more than a pet. He is a real child:

> The mermaid said: "I never knew what it was like when you lived here with your mother and father, I had never seen a little one. He's half like a little man and half—oh, *different!* His arms and legs are so short and white and his head's different—look how soft his hair and skin are! He looks all helpless and not finished yet. He's so new! (142–43)

After he finds out that the boy's mother is dead, the hunter realizes that with the addition of this real child his family is complete: "He smoothed the boy's hair with his big hand and left; when he came home, hours after, his face looked absent and remembering, as if he were back with his own mother and father" (144).

With the boy's arrival, the hunter and the mermaid finally have a family they can believe in: "In a little while they forgot that they had ever lived without the boy." If they are ever reminded about their real and sometimes painful pasts, they need only look at the boy to remind themselves of their sustaining fiction of family. The hunter helps his son to make his own "children's arms," and the mermaid teaches him to tell stories in a voice that sounds "like one of the sea people" (155). The boy accepts his new family as a child too young to remember does: "except for one or two confused, uneasy dreams, all the boy's memories were memories of the mermaid and the hunter; he *knew* that the hunter was his father and the mermaid his mother and had always been" (156–57). The fictional family that the hunter and mermaid have created for him is one which he does not question (162). The hunter and mermaid, however, can remember having been unhappy, and are reminded from time to time of their lonely lives before they created their family. The mermaid is fully aware of the costs involved in belonging to a human family, in contrast to her long ago family under the sea, which she articulates in a very moving passage:

They don't know how to be bored or miserable. One day is one wave, and the next day the next, for the sea people—and whether they're glad or whether they're sorry, the sea washes it away. When my sister died, the next day I'd forgotten and was happy. But if you died, if he died, my heart would break. (170)

With this declaration, the mermaid becomes the heroine of *The Animal Family* because she chooses the land, in all its heartbreaking difference from the sea. Like the bat-poet, she is able, through poetry, to create the supreme fiction of family. With her family complete, she begins, "to talk, and to talk, and to talk as she had never talked before" (165). To the boy, she becomes the highest sort of poet, the storyteller whose fictions are essential to the boy's existence—"there was nothing he liked better than the mermaid's stories" (174). The animal family itself is the mermaid's fiction, a saving one.

The land is better for the mermaid because she is able to have a family, able to experience the possibility of heartbreak. And there appear to be hints that separation looms in the future; the boy is beginning to yearn for the sea just as the mermaid once yearned for the land. Though the hunter and the mermaid tell him that the lynx found him, he "knows" that it's not true. He thinks that the story is part of an amusing game, and soon the hunter and the mermaid come to believe it's a game too. At the end of the book, the roles of parent and child are curiously reversed: the boy tells the truth, "The lynx found me," believing it to be a lie, and the hunter and mermaid tell a lie, "We've had you always," believing it to be the truth.

Randall Jarrell's children's fictions, especially *The Animal Family,* help the reader to understand his or her relationship to that "original composite entity," the family. Although they are "family romances," they transcend simple wish-fulfillment in that they emphasize the making or invention of that family on the part of its members. We have no choice as to the family we are born into, and yet we are not mere victims of circumstance. We must participate actively in making and defining a place for ourselves in that entity by understanding its peculiar jurisprudence, and by understanding that it is a fragile but vital fiction, if we are not to be "separated off." *The Animal Family* and *The Bat-Poet* provide arguments for the usefulness of fiction in helping us make our place both in our particular family "with its own ways and laws" and in the larger community of men, women, and children. Even as we acknowledge that belonging to a family or community is difficult and involves compromise, we see the value of faith in a controlling, supreme fiction. The wish embodied in the epigraph to *The Animal Family*, "Say what you like, but such things do happen—not often, but they do happen" is a wish but not "a blind wish . . . / What the wish wants to see, it sees" (*Complete Poems* 335). While he acknowledges the value of wishes in his children's fiction, Jarrell also argues that mere wishes are not enough; we must make something out of our wishes, as a child makes a family, as a poet makes a poem.

SEVEN

The Lost World
of Childhood

In September 1956, Jarrell wrote to Elizabeth Bishop, saying "I mean to write a real article about your poems. I was crazy about your village story ["In the Village"] in *The New Yorker* too—Peter Taylor said that it was the best thing that had been in *The New Yorker* in years" (413). Jarrell must have been conscious of his borrowing of Bishop's central phrase, "the echo of a scream," when he included it in his poem "In Montecito," written in the summer of 1960—"his first poem in two years" (*Letters* 445), and the first new poem Jarrell composed for the book that was later to become *The Lost World*. Despite Jarrell's initial resistance to his friend Robert Lowell's confessional poems in *Life Studies*, such as "My Last Afternoon with Uncle Devereux Winslow," it is clear that they influenced his work in *The Lost World*. But Jarrell himself notes a greater debt to Bishop. The brilliant autobiographical fiction about a child's perception of her mother's madness that Jarrell so admired is remarkable for what Bishop and Jarrell (outwardly such different poets) share—what Bishop in "Over 2000 Illustrations and a Complete Concordance" calls "infant sight" (*Complete Poems* 59). Bishop suggests in her poem that we must look at the world as children in order to see as true adults; after the speaker of "2000 Illustrations" looks at the nativity scene in the Bible as "a family with pets," she says, "we looked and looked our infant sight away"—maturity, the poem says, comes by virtue of our having first looked at the world from the child's perspective.

In a 1957 letter to Bishop, Jarrell describes what he sees as their affinity:

> I like all of your new poems *so* much, you seem to me to be writing nothing but good poems, something theoretically and practically impossible.
> . . . I like your poetry better than anybody's since the Frost-Stevens-Eliot-Moore generation, so I looked with awed wonder at some phrases feeling to me a little like some of my phrases, in your poems; I felt as if, so to speak, some of my wash-cloths were part of a Modigliani collage, or as if my cat had got into a Vuillard. I think too, that all people who really remember childhood and do it at all right sound alike in some ways. (*Letters* 420)

We must, Bishop and Jarrell agree, look with "infant sight" in order to look it "away"—to reach true maturity. In his excellent book about Bishop, Thomas Travisano says, "To see with infant sight is not to return to childhood, but, far more difficult, to see, through the eyes of experience, with a child's curiosity" (121). Jarrell certainly shares Bishop's devotion to this difficult vision. As Bishop herself said about Jarrell, "we really were in agreement about everything that mattered" ("Inadequate Tribute" 20).

Jarrell's last attempt to gain "infant sight" in order to transcend it, to "really remember childhood" in *The Lost World,* was inspired by an event Mary Jarrell describes in her preface to the 1985 reissue of the volume: "Jarrell's mother sent him an old Christmas card box from the twenties containing the letters he had written her from California when he was twelve" ("The Lost World" ix). Mary Jarrell's description of the letters and an examination of the letters themselves indicate the amount of recollection and, indeed, invention that must have gone into the finished poems; the letters are ordinary, newsy, chatty, and filled with childish versions of Jarrell's characteristic expressions, like "Golly" and "Gee Whiz." They seem happy, even effusive descriptions of mostly mundane events, but like Proust's *madeleine* they seem to have been enough to inspire Jarrell's search for lost childhood. Re-encountering the letters that indicated a childhood paradise led Jarrell to remember what it had really been like to be a child. If, in the children's books, Jarrell embarked upon his prayer of rediscovery, in *The Lost World,* he finds that "the search for childhood paradise leads to its ruins (Kuhn 219). Confronting his own "embarrassing, magical beginnings," he sees the child's world as one that is "potentially far more" than the debased adult world of Greenie Taliaferro's fashionable suburb or of the "Three Bills" at the Plaza hotel. But he also sees that the child's world is "more ignorant and gullible and emotional."

In his Proustian search for lost time, his Wordsworthian search for the lost world of childhood, Jarrell, in his only explicitly autobiographical poems, confronts his own "deeply humiliating" memories. Like many major poems, "The Lost World" and its companion poem "Thinking of the Lost World" are crisis poems. Jarrell's search for childhood paradise, like the farmer's in "Field and Forest," involves taking off everything but a wish, "a blind wish":

> and yet the wish isn't blind,
> What the wish wants to see, it sees.

(335)

In the "Lost World" poems, Jarrell comes to the same recognition Frost comes to in one of Jarrell's favorite poems, "Directive." Encountering the ruined playhouse of the children, Frost's speaker has the astonishing, terrifying revelation that "This was no play house, but a house in earnest." Like Frost, Jarrell comes to realize that his quest for the true grail of childhood results in his finding a "grail-parody"— a broken drinking goblet. As if agreeing with Rilke's Malte who says, "I prayed to rediscover my childhood, and it has come back, and I feel it is just as difficult as it used to be, and that growing older has served no purpose at all" (64), Jarrell's attempt to "drink and be whole again beyond confusion" is an attempt that is necessarily and ironically

doomed. Nevertheless, it is an attempt Jarrell feels he is compelled to
make. We must, he says, find a balance between wishes and truth.

Recalling his own youthful enthusiasm for books in an unpublished
address to an unidentified library association, Jarrell says, "The pages
opened into life or something better than life, into a possibility without
limits." In his essay "Stories," Jarrell says, "A story tells the truth or a
lie—is a wish, or a truth, or a wish modified by a truth. Children ask
first of all: 'Is it a *true* story?' They ask this of the storyteller, but they
ask of the story that it satisfy their wishes" (*Sad Heart* 140). Stories
of pure wish seem primarily lyric, and in a sense impotent; stories of
pure truth seem purely narrative, resembling the "processes of continually increased excitement found in sex and play" (*Sad Heart* 159).
But the greatest stories, Jarrell argues, are those of a wish modified by
a truth, those that contain a dialogue between wishes and truth, the
pleasure principle and the reality principle, childhood and maturity.
Pure wish seems fixed in childhood, encased, like Snow White, in
glass that "encloses":

> As glass does, a womanish and childish
> And doggish universe. We press our noses
> To the glass and wish: the angel- and devilfish
> Floating by on Vine, on Sunset, shut their eyes
> And press their noses to the glass and wish.
>
> (287)

The supreme wish, for Jarrell the child, as the children's books
and his interest in family romance in Kipling show, is the wish to be
adopted. Peter Brooks, in *Reading for the Plot,* notices that the family
romance seems to involve two stages: in the first, both parents are replaced; and in the second, the child, who must inevitably accept the
mother as a real mother, continues to fantasize about replacing the
father. Brooks then notes Roland Barthes's observation "that the child
appears to 'discover' the Oedipus complex and the capacity for con-
structing coherent narrative at the same stage of life" (64). The child,

in short, modifies the adoption wish with the truth that his or her mother is the real mother, but as Freud states in "Family Romances," *"pater semper incertus est."*

In his monologues spoken by aging parents, "Next Day," "The Lost Children," and "Hope," Jarrell detects some of the sources for the child's need for family romance—primarily the uncertainty that adults themselves feel. Adults, faced with their own mortality, feel as the narrator of "Next Day" does, "What I've become / Troubles me even if I shut my eyes" (279). The child, unable to deal with the confusion of adults, must fantasize beings less fallible than parents. For children of unstable families, the confusion of adults is often more pronounced for the child, and these children often replicate their parents' confusion once they reach maturity. The speaker of "Next Day" speaks in seeming oxymorons—"young" and "miserable"; "pretty" and "poor"; "mistaken / Ecstatic, accidental bliss, the blind / happiness"—yet she recognizes that to be an adult is to live with seeming contradictions, by seeing them not so much as chosen, but as outcomes dictated by "The chance of life" (279–80). The speaker of "The Lost Children," haunted by the memories of the children she no longer has—one dead, one grown up—finds it difficult to give up her children's ghosts, and must keep playing a child's game in an attempt to deny her own aging and mortality. But true maturity involves acknowledging one's mortality and living with contradictions.

Mary Jarrell has pointed out in "Ideas and Poems" that Kipling's story "They" was one of the inspirations for "The Lost Children," and, clearly, spectres of children haunt the entire volume. The male narrator of "Hope" is haunted by "a recurrent / Scene from my childhood. / A scene called Mother Has Fainted," and concludes about the scene: "It was as if God were taking a nap." Because of the unreliability of his parents—of both parents, "I have followed in my father's light, faint footsteps"—the speaker suffers confusion in his supposed maturity, primarily a confusion about his sexuality. He replicates his own unstable childhood in his marriage. In his son's dream, "The parents of the apartment fight like lions." He converts the grandfather's clock near the beginning of the poem to a grandmother's clock near the end. Though Mother looms large in the man's late-night interior monologue, so does the absence of a father; indeed, the speaker seems unable to define what the proper role of a father should be. In his feeling that he has, perhaps, married his mother, he feels that he has become his father by incorporating his father's worst characteristics.

Jarrell himself seems to have had trouble accepting the certainty of maternity as well as the uncertainty of paternity. In the "Lost World" poems he confronts the death, and, to a limited extent, the rebirth of the family romance. The poems cover an idyllic (or *idealized*) period in Jarrell's childhood when he lived with a remarkable, aged adoptive family—his paternal grandparents, called Mama and Pop in the poem, and his great-grandmother, Dandeen—in Hollywood, from 1925 to 1926. During this period Jarrell's parents were in the process of getting a divorce, and his mother, Anna, was living in Nashville with his brother, Charles. Jarrell's father, Owen, was presumably a portrait photographer with the Jarrell-Kramer Studio in Long Beach. What is notable in the poems is that both parents, like Jarrell's, are conspicuously absent.

But with his surrogate family of Mama, Pop, and Dandeen, Jarrell seems to have experienced a rare period of domestic security, "of the ways that habit itself makes holy." This secure domestic world, described as the "first Rome of childhood," is reassuring to the young Jarrell; it "guarantee[s] / As so much here does, that the child knows / Who takes care of him, whom he takes care of." Yet it is a security that is certain to be undermined. The adult speaker recognizes, as does the speaker of "Burning the Letters," that "A child has her own faith, a child's." The child has armed himself against his domestic turmoil, but only with "Children's Arms"—"arms that arm for a child's war the child . . ." The secure domesticity of the childhood paradise is continually undermined by the child's growing awareness that his "first Rome" is in decline.

The poems are inspired by the need of the 49-year-old poet to recapture the childhood paradise, but what he actually recaptures is a
paradise on the brink of its disappearance. The period Jarrell turns
to is the period of awakening adolescence, a transition marred by his
parents' marital difficulties, and compounded by his own first glimpse
of "that hard maze . . . that land / That grown men live in"—the world
of work and sex and money:

> The sooty thread
> Up which the laborers feel their way into
> Their wives and houses, is money; the fact of life
> The secret the grownups share . . .
>
> (285)

The child speaker and the adult speaker of the poem are blurred,
sometimes amalgamated, but consistently informed by the adult's
awareness that the childhood Eden, or Arden, is irretrievably lost.
All that remain are "a few dried leaves marked THIS IS THE GREEN-
WOOD." For the child Jarrell of the "Lost World" poems, the veil of
adulthood is beginning to descend on the child "in the midst of play"
(239). Like the Wordsworthian child, the Jarrellian child is capable of
both fear and joy. But Jarrellian childhood cannot really be "enshrined
for future restoration"; it remains encased in Snow White's glass cof-
fin. A product of a society in which the joys of simple childhood are
seen as "just play, just make-believe," Jarrell's remembrances are not of
nature, but of Hollywood: a pink sphinx from a movie set transformed
into a real estate office, or the Allbran billboard. Like the replica of
the Parthenon in Nashville (for which Jarrell served as the model for
the figure of Ganymede when he was eight or nine), all the magic in
Jarrell's childhood world is imitation magic. But if Jarrell's wonderland
is composed of papier-mache, postmodern artifacts, he refuses to dis-
count them entirely. Something valuable may still be reclaimed from
a childhood spent among these Hollywood ruins—a real remembrance
of childhood, the ability to use the child's-eye perspective to make real
maturity possible.

"Child Randall" (as Lowell calls him in *Notebook*) is unquestionably awed by and happy with his surrogate family in his Hollywood wonderland that includes the movie set for the 1925 silent film adaptation of Arthur Conan Doyle's *The Lost World,* replete with its papier-mache dinosaurs and pterodactyls. But at night he dreams of wolves. Beginning to become aware of the impotence of wishes, the incursion of truth, Child Randall begins to suspect that, like so much else in Hollywood, his miraculous, surrogate family is only make-believe. Recognizing that *The Admirable Crichton* is only a play the seniors put on, he feels "undone when an English sail is sighted," and the marooned children are "rescued":

> The island that the children ran is gone.
> The island sang to me: *Believe! Believe!*
> And didn't I know a lady with a lion?
> Each evening as the sun sank, didn't I grieve
> To leave *my* tree house for reality?
>
> (284–85)

Though the immediate reality of the secure, surrogate family is reassuring, "the whole enchanted drawing-room of our progress," the underlying reality is frightening—parents abandon their children, betray them, abuse them, leave them in the forest to die. The tree house is a domestic fantasy like the domestic fantasy of a grandparental family in which Child Randall seeks reassurance regarding his paternity. In the conversations with his grandfather, Pop,

> Pop tells me what I love to hear about,
> His boyhood in Shelbyville. I play
> What he plays, hunt what he hunts, remember
> What he remembers: it seems to me I could stay
> In that dark forest, lit by one fading ember
> Of his campfire forever . . .
>
> (286)

But the "dark forest," as we have seen, is often Kipling's "dark forest full of families" with Mother and Father Wolf lurking in the shadows.

We see in the image of the dark forest the central conflict of "The Lost World"—the conflict between the pastoral dark forest and the terrifying, actual one. The adolescent boy is secure in his domestic paradise, but his security is continually threatened because all his life he has associated family with separation and betrayal. Discovering his sexuality and the hypocrisies of adults, he resists the terrifying dark forest, resists awareness, and plays (or pretends to play) in the pastoral dark forest of make-believe.

The poem turns on its shortest section, "A Night with Lions," in which the child's confusion is heightened by the sexual confusion of approaching adolescence. Jarrell's childish delight at twelve in visiting his "tall, young brown Aunt's" friend who owns the MGM lion is disturbed by his "dream-discovery" of his sexual attraction to the Aunt, an attraction that he confesses is emblematic of his adult sexuality in "Thinking of the Lost World": "My breath comes fast / Whenever I see someone with your skin / Hear someone with your voice." Though he knows, as the attraction suggests, that his childhood is ending, he tries to deny that knowledge through play. But he sees that his play is pretend play. He sees that the lion, Tawny, pretends to play with him, but that he, the child, is the real player; he still says prayers he doesn't believe in, "not at my age." Attendant upon the confusion of his sexual awakening is his recognition of adult hypocrisy, his recognition that adults pretend too:

> Just as we used to,
> I talk to you, you talk to me or pretend
> To talk to me as grown-up people do,
> Of *Jurgen* and Rupert Hughes, till in the end
> I think as a child thinks: "You're my real friend."
>
> (288)

"A Night with Lions" leaves the young speaker questioning his assumptions about the relationship between children and adults, particularly his assumptions about adults' authority and ability to reassure children. The gulf between children and adults widens whenever he confronts one of the secrets the grown-ups share—work or sex or money—but it deepens most profoundly and disturbingly in terms of the ultimate secret, mortality. In another poem about the gulf between youth and age, "The One Who Was Different," the adult speaker, at a funeral, identifies himself with the corpse, like the speaker of "Next Day." But waiting in the wings is a child, represented by the metonymy of her eyes:

> Too young to have learned yet
> What's seen and what's obscene, they look in eagerly
> For this secret the grown-ups have, the secret
> That, shared, makes one a grown-up.
> They look without sympathy or empathy,
> With interest
> Without me.
>
> (318)

The speaker shares the grown-ups' secret, and the awareness of mortality seems to him human, while the child's unawareness makes her seem somehow inhuman, like Donatello's David. "But I identify myself, as always, / With something that there's something wrong with / With something human," says the speaker in what I take to be a statement that sums up Jarrell's poetic philosophy.

However much he does identify himself with something human, he still has a wish to exempt himself from the grown-up secret of death. Speaking about the corpse in the poem, Jarrell's speaker says:

> This is the sort of thing that could happen to anyone
> Except—
> except—
>
> (318)

The manuscripts make explicit what the finished poem only implies: the painful wish "except Randall." But of course, Jarrell must draw back from his impossible wish to be an exception, remarking ironically, "If a man made up his mind / About death, he could do without it."

Confusion about mortality and a feeling of separation from the very humans with whom the poet identifies conspire to make the gulf between youth and age, innocence and experience, and ultimately audience and poet, insurmountable. The horrifying other, the monstrously innocent child, renders Jarrell nearly speechless; he is able only to offer a kind of eloquent inarticulateness: "I feel like the first men who read Wordsworth. / It's so simple, I can't understand it" (317).

If the speaker of "The One Who Was Different" notices primarily the gulf between youth and age, Jarrell in the "Lost World" poems notices the similarities as well: "I have already traveled / Through time to my childhood. It puzzles me / That age is like it." Watching the squirrels, a mockingbird, and a chipmunk (reminiscent of the children's stories), Jarrell concludes that "our end copies our beginning." He can't help asserting, however, that adulthood seems more confused and tarnished than the "calm country" of childhood. In "A Street Off Sunset," the smell of the Vicks VapoRub Factory causes the speaker to leave the reality of factories and adulthood for the tree house in the eucalyptus tree he climbed in childhood. He attempts a nostalgic visit to his remembered paradise, believing it to be pure and unpolluted, but this belief necessitates ridding himself of the lifetime that has transpired between youth and age: "My lifetime / Got rid of, I sit in a dark blue sedan / Beside my great-grandmother in Hollywood" (289). Hollywood, like the tree house, represents a magical world, an emblem of the lost world of childhood. The child is oblivious to the tawdriness of the Hollywood scenery; he delights in the pink sphinx and the Allbran billboard—his imagination turns even the crassly commercial trappings into the subjects of make-believe. By getting rid of the lifetime that knows better, the speaker of the poem can redeem even advertisements.

But "A Street Off Sunset" also makes clear that sorcerers and ogres do indeed haunt the world of make-believe. In a science fiction story the child reads in *Amazing Stories*, "a scientist ready to destroy the world" evokes real worry, and reminds the child of an earlier, infant fear of the cover of *Literary Digest* depicting a World War I fighter plane. The child, unable to finish the story before he is "forced out of life into bed," lies in the dark listening to Aimee Semple Mac-Pherson on a crystal set, "comfortless." The child is beginning to see through the false reassurance of adults; he sees that their comfort is often cold, often nonexistent. Finishing the story the next morning, in which "the good world wins its victory / Over that bad man," he then moves by "unquestioned habit . . . / To and through and from school," until at home he plays a game of dominoes with Dandeen in a mock-communion between age and youth, reminiscent of the earlier mock-communion in the poem in which a spoon of coffee is poured into his milk, "and the milk, transubstantiated, becomes coffee."

The game of dominoes with the great-grandmother underscores the confusion of the child-speaker in his new role as adolescent. He senses that the roles of parent and child are curiously reversed, and, in a sense, feels guilty for wishing to remain a child, when he feels that what is expected of him is to become responsible like an adult. Wanting to stop playing with Dandeen in order to play with his pet rabbit, Reddy, he checks his childish impulse, "relents," and plays her one more game. The adult speaker's voice intrudes at this point in order to evaluate the situation moralistically: "Real remorse hurts me here, now." Biographically, perhaps, the remorse stems from Jarrell's betrayal of his surrogate family in never writing to them after returning to his mother in Nashville. The adult tries to justify this betrayal by saying, "of course / I *was* a child, I missed them so." Justification, a hypocrisy of sorts, is an adult response, one that is painful both because of its dishonesty and its necessity:

> But justifying
> Hurts too: if I could only play you one more game,
> See you all one more time! I think of you dying,
> Forgiving me—or not, it is all the same
> To the forgiven.
>
> (291)

Justification, hypocrisy, forgiveness are depicted as adult responses to seemingly irrational childhood fears. But the "irrational" fears of the actual child Jarrell, are entirely rational. Running to feed his pet rabbit, young Randall observes his grandmother, Mama, killing a chicken for dinner. The rabbit is Randall's ultimate reassuring presence; it "guarantee[s], / As so much here does that the child knows / Who takes care of him, whom he takes care of." The rabbit becomes, however, an emblem of false reassurance. In response to the boy's question, "Mama, you won't ever kill Reddy, will you?" Mama offers the false reassurance that "she'd never / Kill the boy's rabbit, never even think of it." But according to Mary Jarrell, the grandmother did have the rabbit killed and served for dinner after Randall returned to Nashville, and Jarrell's mother told him about it. The rabbit's death, and the cruel way Randall was informed, stand as an indictment of adults' betrayal of children. Though the child has faith in his caretakers, they betray him, so that he doesn't know "who takes care of him." The child's fear for the pet rabbit's fate, of course, is really a fear for his own fate. Worrying about his rabbit in the poem, young Randall says, "Could such a thing / Happen to anything? It could to a rabbit, I'm afraid; / It could to—" The manuscripts make explicit what is only implied in the poem, "It could to Randall, I'm afraid."

The child, in order to survive, attempts to deny this betrayal, and this denial becomes merged with the adult response of hypocrisy:

> And whenever
> I see her in that dark infinite,
> Standing like Judith, with the hen's head in her hand,
> I explain it away, in vain—a hypocrite
> Like all who love.
>
> (292)

In order to remain human, Jarrell must accept the hypocrisies that being human entails: to be human *is* to be something that there's something wrong with. False reassurance on the part of adults is seen as inevitable; adults are hypocrites out of love, a disturbing paradox indeed. Even when it is seemingly benign, however, the false reassurance of adults is a veil the child sees through. Happy endings, apparently, are not enough to assuage the child's fears. At the end of "The Lost World," young Randall is still disturbed by the story of the scientist, and seeks reassurance from Pop who tells him that no scientist could possibly destroy the world, "No that's just play, / Just make-believe." Because the connection has already been drawn in the poem between the sciencefiction story and the first World War, Pop's reassurance itself is troubled. Randall's uneasiness makes Pop uneasy. In a way, Pop, too, is "a hypocrite / Like all who love."

Pop's reassurance is particularly important to young Randall in that Pop is a surrogate father to him. Appropriately, the poem ends with the scene between Pop and Randall in which Randall makes an uneasy peace with his father-figure—a peace that remains qualified and somehow inadequate. At the end of the poem, Child Randall is poised on the brink of adulthood, momentarily appeased, but haunted by the foreboding skies of what is to come at the end of make-believe:

> My universe
> Mended *almost,* I tell him about the scientist. I say,
> "He couldn't really, could he, Pop?" My comforter's
> Eyes light up, and he laughs. "No that's just play,
> Just make-believe," he says. *The sky is gray,*
> We sit there at *the end* of our good day.
> (292–93; emphasis added)

Having tried to rediscover his childhood paradise, Jarrell inevitably encounters its ruins; he finds *the end* of that good day, the twilight of youth set just off Sunset Boulevard. What the poet, admittedly a "nostalgic type," recognizes are the sad limitations of nostalgia. The seemingly benign gray skies at the end of childhood in Hollywood, in 1926, are transformed into the gray skies of a present-day city in "Thinking of the Lost World," where Jarrell "back in Los Angeles" misses the magical Los Angeles of his youth. Children's arms not only fail the child, but they provide little defense for the adult. In the modern "factory planet," all the child's "arrows are lost or broken":

> My knife is sunk in the eucalyptus tree
> Too far for even Pop to get it out,
> And the tree's sawed down. It and the stair-sticks
> And the planks of the tree house are all firewood
> Burned long ago; its gray smoke smells like Vicks.
>
> (336)

Like the speaker of "The Lost Children," Jarrell, the adult, mourns the ruins of paradise, all the while trying to reassure himself that "somehow it still exists," at least as a fiction he may carry with him.

But Jarrell's youthful hands have disappeared; brown-spotted adult's hands have replaced the "smooth / White bitten-fingernailed one[s]." Seeking in the lost world of childhood a sustaining fiction, a romantic source that can be drawn upon in adulthood, he tries to find the same faith one seeks in religion, as exemplified in his statement, "Unless ye become as little children, ye shall not enter the kingdom of art" (*Sad Heart* 95). Discovering the ruins of the children's playhouse, he echoes the father of the afflicted child in Mark 9:24, to his "old self," saying, "I believe. Help thou mine unbelief." Eliot's remark about *In Memoriam* might well be applied to the "Lost World" sequence: "Its faith is a poor one, but its doubt is a very intense experience" (294).

Or perhaps the quality of the faith in *The Lost World* takes on a resonance to which readers were unaccustomed—a faith tested by very intense doubt that manages still, somehow, to exist. Although in Jarrell's unfinished journey back into childhood he did not quite discover or rediscover beliefs strong enough to sustain him, he was able to begin a project of reclamation in which the child's consciousness, "really remembered," rather than sentimentally recalled, could give the poet the ability to "make." The intensity of Jarrell's doubt is perhaps the reason that the ending of "Thinking of the Lost World" has been read in conflicting ways, most notably by John Crowe Ransom who changed his mind about the ending. That ending, I think, is intentionally ambiguous, and neither of Ransom's readings is accurate, though his attempt to deny the bleakness of the poem in his revised reading is a case of the kind of false reassurance criticized in the poem itself. First, I will quote the ending of the poem, and then Ransom's conflicting readings:

> Moving between the first world and the second.
> I hear a boy call, now that my beard's gray:
> "Santa Claus! Hi, Santa Claus!" It is miraculous
> To have the children call you Santa Claus.
> I wave back. When my hand drops to the wheel,
> It is brown and spotted, and its nails are ridged
> Like Mama's. Where's my own hand? My smooth
> White bitten-fingernailed one? I seem to see
> A shape in tennis shoes and khaki riding-pants
> Standing there empty-handed; I reach out to it
> Empty-handed, my hand comes back empty,
> And yet my emptiness is traded for its emptiness,
> I have found that Lost World in the Lost and Found
> Columns whose gray illegible advertisements
> My soul has memorized world after world:
> LOST—NOTHING. STRAYED FROM NOWHERE. NO REWARD.
> I hold in my own hands, in happiness,
> Nothing: the nothing for which there's no reward.
>
> (338)

Now Ransom's first reading, perhaps the more accurate of the two:

> What Rilke and Jarrell had in common was their obsession with their remembered childhoods, beset with terrors as they were; a thing I confess is not at all the picture of my own childhood, so safe and commonplace. But one must acknowledge it; for poetry's sake one may well envy it. The dreams of children, and the stories by the Brothers Grimm which told them of evil; of such as these is the burden of Jarrell's last book from which I quote the last lines. ("Tribute at Yale" 8)

Ransom here seems willing to admit, as Jarrell always was, the "dark forest" of childhood. It seems somehow truer to the spirit of the poems in that it rejects nostalgia and sentimentality. The later Ransom reading seems both sentimental and falsely reassuring, accepting the hypocrisy Jarrell rejects in the poem:

> I felt at first that this was a tragic ending. But I have studied it till I give up that notion. The NOTHING is the fiction, the transformation to which both boy and man are given. That world is not Lost because it never existed: but it is as precious now as ever. I have come to think that Randall was announcing the beginning of his "second childhood." There is nothing wrong about that, to the best of my knowledge. Out of my more extensive acquaintance with this period of life I can say that it begins gently and ends blissfully. And the first stage of it is when sons and daughters bring grandsons and granddaughters to bless and to play with; they make a wonderfully compatible company. . . . Randall in all his adult life was a great lover of children and pets. ("Rugged Way" 181)

Although the "Lost World" poems are an attempt at fiction, they end in emptiness being traded for emptiness. Jarrell was certainly not announcing the period of "second childhood," and his life was certainly neither gentle nor blissful. In 1964, he suffered a severe nervous breakdown; he wrote virtually nothing in the last year of his life; and he had no children of his own, let alone grandchildren. According to Mary Jarrell, Randall was never a real father to her daughters, and he seems to have related to Alleyne's children as a playmate rather than as a grandfather. Though Jarrell was unquestionably a lover of children and pets, he nevertheless remained fully aware of their victimization, and the poems question severely the compatibility of age and youth. Ransom's second reading has its virtues in recognizing Jarrell's attempt to turn a vanishing fiction into a sustaining one, but Jarrell concludes that the fiction is ultimately unsustainable; it amounts to nothing, despite the poet's attempt to hold that nothing in happiness. Like the happiness of the speaker of "Next Day," Jarrell's happiness is continually in danger of becoming a blind happiness that, "bursting, leaves on the palm some soap and water." The concept of a "second childhood," especially as described by Ransom, seems irremediably sentimental. Jarrell was certainly not entering his dotage at the age of fifty. Jarrell's triumph in the "Lost World" poems lies in his ability to "really remember" childhood, and it is a great disservice to read his search for that "house in earnest" in such a revisionist, sentimental manner. The poems have been attacked on the grounds of sentimentality by critics unwilling to appreciate the complexity of Jarrell's vision, and Ransom's apologetic, revised reading seems only to reinforce their case.

Although the adult in the poem does attempt to trade his own emptiness for the more "positive" emptiness of the child, a symbol of potential, that child remains an apparition: "a shape in tennis shoes and khaki riding-pants." Searching for his childhood paradise, the speaker can't help confronting the fact that the paradise is in ruins, and that it never was truly paradisiacal. The triumph of the poem lies in its rejection of nostalgia, in its acknowledgment of the disappearance of childhood, and in its sad wish that childhood, which *is* truly valuable, could really exist as it should. The poem endorses not a retreat from maturity, but an acceptance of maturity, and consequently of humanity —"something that there's something wrong with." Rather than deny change, Jarrell wants to embrace the kinds of change that only works of art can effect, to say with Rilke, "You must change your life." But even as he embraces change, Jarrell is continually mortal, aware of the difficulty of change, especially for the adult:

> You wake up some fine morning, old.
> And old means changed; changed means you wake up new.
>
> (311)

Jarrell argues that we must have faith in the value of our humanity, even though we may often cry out in desperation, "If only, somehow, I had learned to live!" In "The Player Piano" (1965; 354–55), his last completed poem, Jarrell, adopting a characteristic female persona that is really thinly disguised Randall Jarrell, attempts to make peace with the parents, indeed with all the adults, who betrayed him as a child. Confronting his own embarrassing, magical beginnings, as well as his own aging and his increasing awareness of mortality, he tries to forgive the "two babies with their baby" by saying that they were too young to know better. "But justifying hurts too": despite the speaker's attempt to forgive her parents, she cannot finally do so; she knows that their betrayal of her has left her no choice but to watch her Chopin waltz play itself out, mechanically, a half-inch from her fingers.

EIGHT

"Thinking of the Lost World"

The *Lost World* was to be Jarrell's last volume of poetry. On October 14, 1965, on leave from the University of North Carolina hospital, where he was receiving physical therapy on his hand, Randall Jarrell was taking a walk on a dark highway when he was struck by a car and killed. After an investigation by the authorities, his death was ruled an accident. Jarrell's premature death came at a time when he had begun to make major strides in his poetry, when his reputation as a children's author was reaching new heights, and when he had begun to resume his teaching duties in the aftermath of a nervous breakdown. In short, Jarrell died in mid-career. The appearance of *The Complete Poems* in 1969 prompted Helen Vendler to conclude that Jarrell had "put his genius into his criticism and his talent into his poetry" (111), a judgment that is only now being questioned seriously. Just as we may no longer be inclined to accept Vendler's judgment that Robert Lowell is "our greatest contemporary poet" (125), readers of poetry are just beginning to recognize that a considerable amount of Jarrell's genius went into his poetry. Furthermore, significant critical attention has recently recognized Jarrell's genius as a writer for children.

Because children and childhood are Jarrell's finest subjects, a society which tends to devalue childhood is not immediately willing to value his work. Paradoxically, it is just such a society that needs Jarrell's work. For childhood, far from being inherently trivial or sentimental, is the very subject our society needs to confront if it is to understand the consequences of the changes marking this century. Though at first we may have said, like the speaker of "The One Who Was Different," "I feel like the first men who read Wordsworth. / It's so simple, I can't understand it" (317), Jarrell's imaginative writing penetrates and speaks to our age in ways that the work of other members of the so-called "middle generation" does not.

The reasons that Jarrell's reputation has lagged behind those of Lowell, Berryman, and Schwartz are complex. One obvious reason, of course, is that there is, as yet, no major biography of Jarrell; Jarrell was reticent about his private life, and expressed his desire not to be the subject of a biography, a wish that Mary Jarrell has seen fit to honor.[1] But the more important reasons for the relative critical neglect of Jarrell have more to do with our received critical and cultural values.

Two recent studies, Bruce Bawer's *The Middle Generation: The Lives and Poetry of Delmore Schwartz, Randall Jarrell, John Berryman, and Robert Lowell* and Jeffrey Meyers's *Manic Power: Robert Lowell and His Circle,* attempt to fit Jarrell's life and work into the popular but suspect mythology of a doomed generation of poets. Both critics' arguments, which are inherently Procrustean, break down when they encounter Jarrell. In Bawer's book, one comes across passage after passage in which Jarrell is cited as the "exception," such as "Even Jarrell, who seems to have had a comparatively normal and happy home life, is reported to have said that he shared Hamlet's view of remarriage" or "What does seem probable is that in all the Middle Generation poets' lives, except for that of Jarrell, there was a good deal of repressed homosexuality" (31). Meyers's book is more deceptive; although the jacket copy reads, "As a group, Robert Lowell, Randall Jarrell, John Berryman, and Theodore Roethke were eccentric, unpredictable, unfaithful, alcoholic, violent, and insane," the passage in the text itself reads,

Lowell, Jarrell, Berryman, and Roethke seemed trapped by the same
tragic pattern. They rivalled the previous generation of novelists and
poets in depth of genius and artistic achievement, and surpassed them
in the extremity of pain and authority of suffering. *Lowell, Berryman and
Roethke* were eccentric, unpredictable, unfaithful; alcoholic, violent and
insane. (12; emphasis added)

Although Jarrell was clearly an eccentric, there is absolutely no evidence of the kind of chronic infidelity, alcoholism, violence, or insanity
that characterized the other poets' lives, and Meyers is grudgingly
forced to admit this throughout his study. When his attention turns
to Jarrell ("Jarrell, who did not drink, seemed stable and even in-
vulnerable to disaster"), he immediately follows his admission with
speculation passed off as gospel ("But he too broke down and attempted
suicide in 1964, at the age of 50, and killed himself the following
year.") (16). Jarrell did "break down" in 1964, at least partially as a
result of what would be categorized by today's standards as psychiatric
malpractice; he was treated over long-distance telephone by a psychiatrist who prescribed the relatively new drug Elavil (an anti-depressant)
without properly monitoring the dosage. Jarrell also attempted suicide
in April 1965 when he was residing in the psychiatric ward at Chapel
Hill where he was being treated for a manic episode brought on by the
drug. But Meyers's speculation that Jarrell finally committed suicide
is passed off as a fact, without supporting documentation, when, at
least according to official records, Jarrell's death was ruled accidental.
The only reliable witness who could put an end to the speculation con-
cerning Jarrell's death, Jarrell himself, is dead. Since the dead cannot
be libelled, Meyers is free to express his opinion as fact without fear
of retribution, but in doing so, he comes close to violating the ethics
of responsible scholarship, which should acknowledge the deep and
perhaps permanent ambiguity that enshrouds Jarrell's death.

Jarrell's poetry lacks the bombastic, grand style of Lowell's work, and
it lacks the tortured syntax and verbal inventiveness of Berryman's

best work. But its power is a narrative patience, a tender yet realistic view of humanity, and a concern for the lives of the powerless, particularly children and women. In terms of its humanity, its moral attractiveness, it is a poetry that speaks more directly to our needs than the pyrotechnical displays of Lowell and Berryman that occupy more esteemed places in the canon. In a critical but perceptive essay/review in *The American Scholar,* James Dickey identifies the different approaches to poetry exemplified by Berryman's *77 Dream Songs* and Jarrell's *The Lost World:*

> The difference is absolutely fundamental. . . . [Jarrell] is primarily interested in the reader's *having* the experience the poem is trying to have, that the writer is attempting to repossess for himself. The poem is intended as no more than a pane of glass—perhaps with slight powers of magnification—through which the reader enters the depicted situation to live and learn from it as he is able. In contrast [Berryman's poetry] is fascinated by its own verbal surface, by its sheer linguistic possibilities, its syntactical permutations and combinations, its manipulative prestidigitorial promises. ("Orientations" 646)

Dickey goes on to argue that although each poet is limited by his commitment to carrying his method to extremes, the different methods represent the "primary ways" of American poetry:

> The primary ways are Jarrell's—a total commitment to experience and the attempt to find a mode by which words may seem to efface themselves and allow the experience to stand magically in the place where they formerly were—and Berryman's way of idiosyncratic artifice, a method that strives to raise the ultimate Construct above mannerism into style. . . . American poetry will surely be determined for some time by which lead is followed, which man most successfully used. (658)

Without denigrating the real achievement of Berryman or Lowell, I would argue that Jarrell's way is morally superior. Jarrell's method risks sentimentality, and even bathos, but that is the risk of great poetry—certainly it is a risk taken by Jarrell's poetic heroes, Wordsworth, Frost, and Rilke. To borrow Jarrell's critical terminology and method, "in a lifetime of standing out in thunderstorms" he was struck by lightning in a number of instances. My list of Jarrell's indispensible work would include "90 North," "Eighth Air Force," "Moving," "A Quilt-Pattern," Rilke's "The Grown-up" (if I may admit a translation to the list), "The Lost World," and "Thinking of the Lost World" (roughly the half-a-dozen instances that make a good poet). I would also argue that lightning struck with *The Animal Family*. Though these achievements may not equal *The Prelude* or *The Duino Elegies,* or such quintessential Frost as "Home Burial," there is nothing in Lowell's or Berryman's ouevre that rivals those achievements either.

Most of the contemporary reviews criticizing *The Lost World* were not as thoughtful and intelligent as Dickey's, and they lacked the convincing wit that characterized Jarrell's negative reviews. The most notorious, by Joseph Bennett, concluded, "His work is trashy, and thoroughly dated; prodigiousness encouraged by an indulgent and sentimental Mamaism; its overriding feature is doddering infantilism" (24). Not much kinder was Paul Fussell's attack on "[Jarrell's] monotonous mannerism, attached now too often to the mere chic of sentimental nostalgia and suburban pathos," in which he describes the poem "The Lost World" as "a self-indulgent reminiscence of a Los Angeles boyhood, which is obvious and dull, full of slick ironies and pulled punches" (31). Irvin Ehrenpreis called the poems "odd childhood experiences sentimentally recalled. Conventional nostalgia, conventional pathos, the self-pity of a man who has put early innocence in the place of moral judgment—these are hardly enough to supply an interesting shape for Mr. Jarrell's miscellaneous lines" (167).

But Jarrell's last poetry, autobiographical without being confessional, technically superb without calling undue attention to its formal inventiveness, is neither sentimental nor nostalgic. It is part of a humane enterprise on Jarrell's part to reach an audience that is suspicious of poetry—an attempt to get readers to see the truth about childhood, to help them overcome the limitation of their nostalgic adult impulses to trivialize childhood either as a wholly innocent paradisia-cal time that should be put aside and forgotten or as a bankrupt state of ignorance. In Wordsworthian terms, Jarrell's poetry wishes to en-shrine childhood "for future restoration"; yet it is also a poetry that attempts to look upon the world "not as in the hour of thoughtless youth / But hearing oftentimes the still, sad music of humanity."

One way to measure Jarrell's vision and achievement is to read it alongside work by his contemporaries. If the Jarrellian child resembles the heroic Wordsworthian child, whose connection with nature en-ables it to truly become the father to the man, Lowell's child re-calls the prodigy of the Intimations Ode, the confined child, the little actor: "I was a stuffed toucan / With a bibulous, multicolored beak" (Lowell, *Life Studies* 61). Furthermore, the cult of personality that is preeminent in Lowell's later work, the tendency to mediate im-portant national and world events through the prism of the famous Lowell personality, resembles the egotistical ridiculous more than it does the sublime. Helen Vendler may admire the slack pseudo-sonnets of Lowell's later career, but few others do. And Berryman's Henry is an unreconstructed child, childish in the way Jarrell's child is not. His minstrel-show ethics pave the way for the degeneration of Berryman's poetry into a mere alcoholic obsession with *Love & Fame*. Berryman's horror at his father's suicide and his clinging to a decidedly unhealthy relationship with his mother into "maturity" never allowed him to begin to assimilate valuable childhood experience into his work.

The Bawer and Meyers studies, by leaching these poets of their uniqueness, are themselves fulfilled prophecies of how our culture's values are flawed. The popularity of the mythology of the doomed poet indicts a culture Jarrell saw as becoming "essentially periodical," one in which we smother individuality by glorifying celebrity. "Tomorrow morning," says Jarrell in "The Obscurity of the Poet," "some poet may, like Byron, wake up to find himself famous—for having written a novel, for having killed his wife; it will not be for having written a poem" (*Poetry and the Age* 15). And as Neil Postman, Marie Winn,

Christopher Lasch and others argue, the reach of periodical culture is extensive; it not only undermines the individual but it transforms the family, and particularly the position of the child within the family, in ways that are far from salutary.

In "Children Selecting Books in a Library," the child looks to books in order to define his relationship with the "capricious infinite," but in "Carnegie Library, Juvenile Division" the books do not provide an adequate definition: "We learned to understand, but not to change." In the revised version of "Children Selecting Books," change comes to those "not to themselves endeared." Similarly, the eternally childish woman at the Washington Zoo cries for a change she is powerless to enact. Jarrell himself prays for transformation in his work, and comes to see that change is the vehicle of real maturity. It is not the creature of that false maturity that erects a nostalgic view of childhood, but the transformation that follows the long struggle to see childhood as it actually is. Because society conspires to rob us of our actual childhoods, the mature adult who wishes to draw on the valuable first poetic instance must perform a precarious balancing act, must attempt to hold what may seem "nothing" in happiness, must, against the odds, attempt to become "once a child" without reverting to childishness.

Jarrell's poetics, inextricably linked to his view of childhood, is clearly critical of the enshrinement of periodical culture, which exalts the kitsch of our times by extending a solipsism that is "egoistic and unloving" from cradle to grave. To read Jarrell's image of childhood as a key to unlocking some personal pathological disturbance is to misread an aspect for the whole.

Childhood is not something that healthy adults "get over." That so many twentieth-century adults do see childhood as a pathological site is another symptom of what Alice Miller describes as the societally sanctioned "power adults wield over children" (6). In Miller's view, traditional psychoanalysis, which posits the child as a guilty victim "is more likely to conceal than to reveal the sexual and narcissistic abuse the patient experienced as a child" (7). Only when "the anger of early

childhood and the ensuing grief have been experienced" can "affirmative feelings, which are not based on denial or feelings of duty or guilt
. . . emerge" (23). In short, one must "really remember" childhood
in order to distinguish "affirmative, more mature feelings" from "the
small child's unconditional, dependent, all-forgiving, and therefore
tragic love for his or her parents" (Miller, *Thou Shalt Not* 23).

Affirmative, more mature feelings are exactly what Jarrell sought.
His quest, in the end, must be seen as a quest for maturity and
real change. Of course this journey—and Jarrell's lifelong wish for
change—was perilous, and, unfortunately, it was cut short. But, as
his September 1965 letter (one of his last) to Robert Penn Warren
shows, it is a quest which explicitly rejects mental illness and endorses
maturity:

> I've been home from the hospital almost two months, and am my usual
> self again and very glad to be—I've always wanted to change, but not to
> change into what you become when you're mentally ill. . . . I haven't
> written any poems, but I've been thinking so much about the passage of
> time, and what it's like to live a certain number of years in the world,
> that I think it's certain to turn into some poems in the long run. (*Letters*
> 515–16)

Clearly Jarrell does not endorse the idea that madness is necessary for
his poetry. The sad irony of the last line of "Seele im Raum," "To own
an eland! That's what I call life!" is that the speaker's nostalgia for
mental illness is no answer—neither the life of mental illness with the
eland nor the stark, unimaginative life without it are what most of us
would call life. Forgetting or retreating into madness provide no real
answer for Jarrell; remembering and affirming the positive and healthy
aspects of the imagination matter above all.

Writing to Maurice Sendak during the same month, Jarrell expresses
his pleasure with Sendak's "decorations" for *The Animal Family* and
speaks of what makes the two artists ideal collaborators:

> I feel so lucky and grateful to have had your pictures for both the *Animal
> Family* and *The Bat-Poet*. . . . What you say about *The Animal Family*

makes me feel awfully good. I'd like to have it a good book, and when
people like you like it as you do—people with so much understanding
and remembrance of childhood, so much magic and imagination of their
own—it makes me hope that the book really is what it ought to be.
(*Letters* 514)

In his essay "The Taste of the Age" (1958), Jarrell satirizes the
children's book-publishing industry:

> As one reads one sees before one, as if in a vision, the children's book
> of the future: a book that, pressed, says: *I'm your friend;* teaches the
> child that Crime Does Not Pay; does not exceed thirty words; can be
> used as a heating-pad if the electric blanket breaks down; and has three-
> dimensional illustrations dyed with harmless vegetable coloring matter
> and flavored with pure vanilla. I can hear the children of the future
> crying: "Mother, read us another vanilla book!" (*Sad Heart* 31–32)

Maurice Sendak's criticism of the children's book-publishing industry in his 1964 Caldecott Medal acceptance speech recalls Jarrell's
criticism, and illuminates our received notions about Jarrell, not just
Jarrell the children's author, but Jarrell the poet, novelist, and critic
for adults:

> The realities of childhood put to shame the half-true notions in some
> children's books. These offer a gilded world unshadowed by the least
> suggestion of conflict or pain, a world manufactured by those who cannot
> —or don't care to—remember the truth of their own childhood. Their
> expurgated vision has no relation to the way real children live.
>
> I suppose these books have some purpose—they don't frighten adults,
> those adults who cling to the great nineteenth-century fantasy that paints
> childhood as an eternally innocent paradise. These so-called children's
> books are published under false colors, for they serve only to indulge
> grownups. They are passed from adult to adult, for they could only be
> loved by adults who have a false and sentimental recollection of child-
> hood. (153)

What both of these essays deplore is a deep-seated, culturally sanctioned trivialization of childhood, a condescension to actual children;

as Jarrell notes in his Christina Stead essay, adult misconceptions about
childhood arise from an adult's inability (or unwillingness) to remember what childhood is really like. Sendak indicts adults in his speech
for not taking children's literature seriously, an indictment that obviously deserves to be reiterated when critics like Meyers assume *a priori*
that writing for children is inferior to writing for adults, implying that
children are somehow not fully human. Speculating about Jarrell's reaction to an encouraging letter from Lowell, Meyers concludes that
Jarrell was depressed that "he had failed to develop as an artist and
was now writing children's books that signalled a regressive retreat
from adult concerns" (50). Meyers, of course, disregards the fact that
at least one of Jarrell's children's books, *The Animal Family*, is widely
regarded as a modern classic, and that Jarrell's writing for children
was instrumental in helping him to write poetry again, indeed the most
mature and effective poetry of his career.

As we have seen, Jarrell's prayer of rediscovery, his desire to remember childhood, not childishly, but with the mature, affirmative feelings
of a "once a child," was difficult. If we agree with Denis Donoghue
that the "raw wounds" of the early work do not represent Jarrell at his
best, we must also see that, in terms of Jarrell's development as a poet,
it was necessary that his anger and grief be expressed. The poet who
had said in his youth "existence is guilt enough" (*Blood* 21) could not
yet offer us a way of "making"; he could merely describe. In his early
work, Jarrell is caught up in a troubling bind. He wishes, it seems,
to transcend the excesses of modernism: "how can anyone," he asks,
"fail to see that the excesses of modernist poetry are the necessary
concomitants of the excesses of late-capitalist society" (*Kipling, Auden*
82). But Jarrell in his youth writes within the discourse of modernism.
The early poetry—even the finest early poetry such as "90 North"—
can find no way out of modernist fragmentation other than nihilistic
despair.

Jarrell abandons the Marxist rhetoric of this critique of modernism,
but he never abandons his wish that poetry might, at least, shore up

the fragments, that poetry, rather than serving as a concomitant to our social excesses, can provide a criticism of those excesses and can become, by example, a partial solution to them. If this view seems essentially Arnoldian, it is also, in a way, postmodern, as Jerome Mazzaro suggests (82–100). Although he shares the Arnoldian view that poetry is a "criticism of life," Jarrell does not, finally, endorse a retreat from life.

Robert Pattison, in *The Child Figure in English Literature,* suggests that the failure of Wordsworth's late poetry results from Wordsworth adopting an orthodox view of childhood diametrically opposed to his early, "heretical" view. But Jarrell, late in his career, comes to reject an orthodoxy he knows to be egoistic, unloving, solipsistic, and ultimately nihilistic. Noting that, "like Wordsworth, Jarrell wanted to define and express the beauty and significance of ordinary life in a language actually spoken by men," Suzanne Ferguson suggests that in some of his late poems "it is probably not too much to claim that [Jarrell] succeeded better than his master" (*Poetry* 229). Though it is patently absurd to suggest that Jarrell was as great a poet as Wordsworth, at least in the tenacity of his belief in the value of childhood, a belief that was and is threatened by the excesses of our culture, Jarrell does, perhaps, surpass his master.

Unless we remain blinded by our modern orthodoxies about childhood, orthodoxies that see the child as guilty, pitiful, and monstrous, that see childhood as something to be "gotten over," we cannot call Jarrell's later poetry sentimental. In a world in which the football star Big Daddy Lipscomb's death from a heroin overdose can be dismissed as a "NETWORK DIFFICULTY," the ordinary fallout of a discontinuous postmodern culture, Jarrell nevertheless affirms the necessity of tapping the deep sources of childhood. His poetry offers a way of rediscovering the universal language of the unconscious that might unite us as human beings rather than leaving us disunited fragments of humanity. The rediscovery and use of the child's-eye perspective may be joyful, as in young Jarrell's delight in "children's arms," or it may be frightening, as in the intimations of mortality he experiences watching "Mama" wring the chicken's neck. The ability to remember childhood may point out our failures as adults or expose us to terrors we might prefer to keep repressed (as in "Gleaning"), but it will not permit us to dismiss those terrors as so much static on the television.

It is sadly ironic that Jarrell's poetic journey back to his own childhood was to be his last work. The poet who had spent much of his life and work cataloguing the widespread abuse and devaluation of the child in our times ended his career poised on the brink of discovery. For Jarrell, it seemed that poetry might become a way out of childhood into maturity, not the false maturity of the adult who tries to forget childhood because of its misery and humiliation, but the true maturity which remembers both the difficulties and the rewards, the tears and the joy, at the heart of the lost world of childhood.

List of Books Destroyed by Fire

Note: Randall's library was destroyed when he was a senior in high school and he prepared this list for insurance purposes. Prices are omitted.

Title	*Author*
Madame Bovary	Flaubert
Sanctuary	Faulkner
Point Counterpoint	Huxley
Antic Hay	Huxley
In Our Times [*sic*]	Hemingway
The Education of Henry Adams	Henry Adams
Swann's Way	Proust
In a Budding Grove	Proust
Philosophy	Bertrand Russell
Success	Feuchtwanger
As I Lay Dying	Faulkner
Fantasia of the Unconcious [*sic*]	D. H. Lawrence
Alice in Wonderland	Lewis Carroll
The Lower Depths	Gorki
The Women at Point Sur	Jeffers
Arabia Deserta	Doughty
The Last and First Men	

(*continued*)

The Decline of the West	Spangler [*sic*]
The Golden Bough	Fraser [*sic*]
The Hamlet of A. MacLeish	Archibald MacLeish
Salammbo	Flaubert
The Wild Duck	Ibsen
Homer's "Odyssey"	
Thus Spake Zarathustra	Nietzsche
Creative Evolution	Bergson
The Food of the Gods	Wells
The Cherry Orchard	Chekov [*sic*]
The Ugly Duchess	Feuchtwanger
Poems	Elliot [*sic*]
Rubiyait [*sic*]	Omar Khayyam
Jurgen	Cabell
The Silver Stallion	Cabell
Collected Poems of Robert Browning	
The Idiot	Dostoievsky
War and Peace	Tolstoy
De Maupassant's Short Stories	Collected Edyion [*sic*]
The Torrents of Spring	Hemingway
Memoirs of a Fox-Hunting Man	Sassoon
Arrowsmith	Lewis
The Patriot's Progress	Henry Williamson
Crime and Punishment	Dostoievsky
Her Privates We	
Little Caesar	Burnett
The Forsyte Saga	Galsworthy
Kristin Lavrandsdatter	
My Antonia Cather [*sic*]	
The Green Meadow	Roberts
Enfants Terrible	Cocteau
Collected Verse of Lewis Carroll	
Peter Whiffle	Carl Van Vechten
Anna Karenina	Tolstoy
Gallions Reach	Tomlinson

The Temptation of St. Anthony	Flaubert
Holiday	Phillip Barry
All Quiet on the Western Front	
Gulliver's Travels	
The Nature of the Physical World	Eddington
He Who gets Slapped	Andreyeo
Introduction to Mathematical Philosophy	Russell
The Three Musketeers	
Twenty Years After	
Huckleberry Finn	
Bible	
Bible	
Science and Health	Eddy
Bible Stories	
Tales of Shakespeare	Lamb
Best Stories to Tell Children	

Notes

Chapter One

1. All references to Jarrell's poems are from *The Complete Poems* (1969) unless otherwise indicated.

2. Most of the biographical information in this chapter is derived from a personal interview with Mary Jarrell on 12 June 1984 and from documents provided by her at the interview.

Chapter Two

1. Helen Hagenbuchle in *The Black Goddess* explores the image of the horrid nurse at length, but her Jungian concentration on the archetypal feminine in Jarrell causes her to explain the image in terms of the child's separation from the mother rather than in terms of the abuse the children suffer.

Chapter Three

1. The popularity of extraterrestrials in the fantasy lives of modern children should be obvious. For Jarrell, the wish to be adopted by alien beings was lifelong. In *Pictures* both the narrator and Gottfried Rosenbaum want to have visitors from a space ship make them "pets."

Chapter Five

1. Russell Fowler's article "Charting the Lost World: Rilke's Influence on Jarrell" gives an excellent account of the importance of Jarrell's Rilke translations as an influence on the later poetry.

2. Inexplicably, Helen Hagenbuchle says that Jarrell was attracted to Donatello's David because the artist "added" the beheading to the Biblical account, and she makes much ado about the Jungian ramifications of this "added" detail. My Bible (I Samuel 17:51) has David beheading Goliath with Goliath's sword.

Chapter Six

1. Jarrell quotes the infant babe passage of *The Prelude,* ironically, in "A Sad Heart at the Supermarket" (67). Mary Jarrell says that Jarrell spoke of writing a long piece on *The Prelude* before his death (interview with the author, 12 June 1984).

2. Griswold's study is particularly good in describing the conversation between the texts and the illustrations.

3. Though not published until 1976, *Fly by Night* is Jarrell's penultimate children's book, not his last. The reason for the long delay may be partially explained by Sendak's difficulty in illustrating the book. Griswold gives an excellent account of this difficulty.

4. David's dog is named Reddy, which was the name of Jarrell's pet rabbit whose death the child fears in "The Lost World." Curiously, Jarrell here gives the name to a dog and has him dream that he has killed a rabbit. The image of a loved one killing animals is prevalent in the poetry. One reason for its recurrence in Jarrell's work, perhaps, is that according to Mary Jarrell, Jarrell's grandmother did have his rabbit killed and cooked for dinner, a fact Jarrell was aware of because his mother told him about it (interview with the author, 12 June 1984).

5. It seems to me that it is significant that the cardinal is a father. Possibly, the bat is disturbed by seeing a nurturing father, something he and Jarrell seem not to have had.

6. "The Chipmunk's Day" is the only poem from *The Bat-Poet* that Jarrell

chose to exclude from *The Lost World*. Clearly it is the least interesting of the bat's poems.

Chapter Eight

1. The publication of Mary Jarrell's edition of *Randall Jarrell's Letters* in 1985 made available much biographical information previously unavailable. William Pritchard's study *Randall Jarrell: A Literary Life*, which I read after this book went to press, though not an authorized biography, makes even more available.

Works Consulted

Essays included in Suzanne Ferguson, ed., *Critical Essays on Randall Jarrell,* are cited as *Crit. Essays.* Essays included in Robert Lowell et al., eds., *Randall Jarrell, 1914–1965,* are cited as *RJ.*

Original Works by Randall Jarrell

About Popular Culture. Winston-Salem, N.C.: Palaemon Press, 1981.

The Animal Family. Decorations by Maurice Sendak. New York: Pantheon, 1965.

The Bat-Poet. Illus. Maurice Sendak. New York: Macmillan, 1964.

Blood for a Stranger. New York: Harcourt, 1942.

The Complete Poems. New York: Farrar, 1969.

Fly by Night. Illus. Maurice Sendak. New York: Farrar, 1976.

The Gingerbread Rabbit. Illus. Garth Williams. New York: Macmillan, 1964.

Kipling, Auden, & Co. New York: Farrar, 1981.

Little Friend, Little Friend. New York: Dial, 1945.

"Looking back in my mind I see . . ." *Southern Review* 1 (1935): 85–86. Another version, entitled "The Elementary Scene," was published in *The Woman at the Washington Zoo* (1960).

Losses. New York: Harcourt, 1948.

The Lost World. New York: Macmillan, 1965.

Pictures from an Institution. New York: Knopf, 1954.

Poetry and the Age. New York: Knopf, 1953.

The Poetry of Randall Jarrell. New York: Jeffrey Norton, 1963. Cassette tape no. 23178. (Available from Watershed Foundation, Washington, D.C.)

"The Rage for the Lost Penny." In *Five Young American Poets*. Norfolk, Conn.: New Directions, 1940.

Randall Jarrell's Letters: An Autobiographical and Literary Selection. Ed. Mary Jarrell. Boston: Houghton, 1985.

A Sad Heart at the Supermarket. New York: Atheneum, 1962.

Selected Poems. New York: Knopf, 1955.

The Seven-League Crutches. New York: Harcourt, 1951.

The Third Book of Criticism. New York: Farrar, 1969.

The Woman at the Washington Zoo. New York: Atheneum, 1960.

Works Edited by Randall Jarrell

The Anchor Book of Stories. New York: Anchor, 1958.

The Best Short Stories of Rudyard Kipling. New York: Hanover House, 1961.

The English in England (Kipling). New York: Hanover House, 1963.

In the Vernacular: The English in India (Kipling). New York: Doubleday, 1963.

Six Russian Novels. New York: Anchor, 1963.

Translations by Randall Jarrell

Goethe's Faust, Part I. New York: Farrar, 1976.

The Golden Bird and Other Fairy Tales of the Brothers Grimm. New York: Macmillan, 1962.

The Rabbit Catcher and Other Fairy Tales of Ludwig Bechstein. New York: Macmillan, 1962.

The Three Sisters, by Anton Chekhov. New York: Macmillan, 1969.

Secondary Sources

Adams, Charles M. "A Bibliographical Excursion with Some Biographical Footnotes on Randall Jarrell." *Bulletin of Bibliography* 28 (1971): 79–81.

———. *Randall Jarrell: A Bibliography*. Chapel Hill: University of North Carolina Press, 1958.

———. "A Supplement to *Randall Jarrell: A Bibliography*," *Analects* (Greensboro, N.C.) 1 (Spring 1961): 49–56.

Arendt, Hannah. "Randall Jarrell." In *RJ*, 3–9.

Ariès, Philippe. *Centuries of Childhood*. Trans. Roger Baldrick. New York: Vintage, 1962.

Bawer, Bruce. *The Middle Generation: The Lives and Poetry of Delmore Schwartz, Randall Jarrell, John Berryman, and Robert Lowell*. Hamden, Conn.: Archon Books, 1986.

Beck, Charlotte. "Unicorn to Eland: The Rilkean Spirit in the Poetry of Randall Jarrell." In *Crit. Essays*, 191–202.

———. *Worlds and Lives: The Poetry of Randall Jarrell*. Port Washington, N.Y.: Associated Faculty Press, 1983.

Bennett, Joseph. "Utterances, Entertainment and Symbols." *New York Times Book Review*, 18 April 1965, 24.

Bishop, Elizabeth. *The Collected Prose*. Ed. Robert Giroux. New York: Farrar, 1984.

———. *The Complete Poems: 1927–1979*. New York: Farrar, 1984.

———. "An Inadequate Tribute." In *RJ*, 20–21.

Booth, Philip. "Jarrell's Lost World." In *RJ*, 22–25.

Brooks, Cleanth. "Jarrell's 'Eighth Air Force.'" In *RJ*, 26–32.

Brooks, Peter A. *Reading for the Plot: Design and Intention in Narrative*. New York: Vintage, 1985.

Bryant, J. A. *Understanding Randall Jarrell*. Columbia: University of South Carolina Press, 1986.

Chappell, Fred. "The Longing to Belong." *Field* 35 (Fall 1986): 23–29.

Children's Literature Review 6 (1983): 151–68.

Coles, Robert. *The Moral Life of Children*. Boston: Houghton, 1987.

Coveney, Peter. *The Image of Childhood*. Rev. ed. Baltimore: Penguin, 1967.

Cross, Richard K. "Jarrell's Translations: The Poet as Elective Middle European." In *Crit. Essays:* 310–20.

———. "You Must Change Your Life." *Parnassus* 11, no. 1 (Spring–Summer 1983): 264–69.

Dickey, James. "Orientations." *American Scholar* 34 (1965): 646–58.

———. "Randall Jarrell." In *RJ:* 33–48.

Donoghue, Denis. "*The Lost World.*" In *RJ:* 49–62.

Ehrenpreis, Irvin. "Poetry Without Despair." *Virginia Quarterly Review* 42 (1966): 165–67.

Eliot, T. S. *Selected Essays: New Edition.* New York: Harcourt, 1964.

Emerson, Ralph Waldo. "Nature." In *Selections from Ralph Waldo Emerson,* ed. Stephen Whicher, 21–56. Boston: Houghton, 1957.

Erikson, Eric H. *Childhood and Society.* 2d ed. New York: Norton, 1963.

Fein, Richard. "Randall Jarrell's World of War." In *Crit. Essays:* 149–62.

Ferguson, Frances. "Randall Jarrell and Flotations of Voice." In *Crit. Essays:* 163–75.

Ferguson, Suzanne. "The Death of Randall Jarrell: A Problem in Legendary Biography." *Georgia Review* 37 (1983): 866–76.

———. "Narrative and Narrators in the Poetry of Randall Jarrell." *South Carolina Review* 17 (Fall 1984): 71–82.

———. *The Poetry of Randall Jarrell.* Baton Rouge: Louisiana State University, 1972.

———. "Randall Jarrell," *Dictionary of Literary Biography* 48 (1986): 246–66.

———. "To Benton With Love and Judgment." In *Crit. Essays,* 272–83.

Ferguson, Suzanne, ed. *Critical Essays on Randall Jarrell.* Boston: G.K. Hall, 1983.

Flynn, Richard. "Happy Families Are All Invented: Randall Jarrell's Fiction for Children." *Children's Literature* 16 (1988): 109–25.

———. "Memoirs of a Haunted Childhood." Review of *Randall Jarrell's Letters. The Bloomsbury Review* 5, no. 11 (September 1985): 3, 16.

Fowler, Russell T. "Charting the 'Lost World': Rilke's Influence on Jarrell." *Twentieth-Century Literature* 30 (1985): 100–122.

———. "Randall Jarrell's 'Eland': A Key to Motive and Technique in His Poetry." In *Crit. Essays:* 176–90.

Freud, Anna, and Dorothy Burlingham. *War and Children*. New York: Medical War Books, 1943.

Freud, Sigmund. "Family Romances." In *The Standard Edition of the Complete Psychological Works of Sigmund Freud*, trans. James Strachey, 9: 237–41. London: Hogarth, 1959.

————. *The Interpretation of Dreams*. Trans. James Strachey. New York: Avon, 1965.

Frost, Robert. *The Poetry of Robert Frost*. Ed. Edward Connery Lathem. New York: Holt, 1969.

Fussell, Paul. "How to Sing of a Diminished Thing." *Saturday Review* 48 (3 July 1965): 30–32.

Graham, W. S., and Hayden Carruth. "Jarrell's 'Losses': A Controversy." *Poetry* 72 (1948): 302–11.

Griswold, Jerome. *The Children's Books of Randall Jarrell*. Athens: University of Georgia Press, 1988.

————. "Mother and Child in the Poetry and Children's Books of Randall Jarrell." Ph.D. diss., University of Connecticut, 1979.

Hagenbuchle, Helen. *The Black Goddess: A Study of the Archetypal Feminine in the Poetry of Randall Jarrell*. Bern: Francke Verlag, 1975.

Hallberg, Robert von. *American Poetry and Culture, 1945–1980*. Cambridge, Mass.: Harvard University Press, 1985.

Hamilton, Ian. *Robert Lowell: A Biography*. New York: Random, 1982.

Hartman, Geoffrey. *The Unmediated Vision: An Interpretation of Wordsworth, Hopkins, Rilke, and Valery*. New York: Harcourt, 1966.

Jarrell, Mary. Afterword to Goethe's *Faust, Part One*, trans. Randall Jarrell. New York: Farrar, 1976.

————. "The Group of Two." In *RJ*, 274–98.

————. "Ideas and Poems." *Parnassus* 5 (Fall–Winter 1976): 213–30.

————. Introduction to *Jerome: The Biography of a Poem*, by Randall Jarrell. New York: Grossman, 1971.

————. Liner Notes to "Randall Jarrell's *The Bat-Poet* Read by the Author." New York: Caedmon Cassette, 1972.

————. "The Lost World: Twenty Years After." Foreword to *The Lost World: New Poems*, by Randall Jarrell, ix–xvi. New York: Macmillan, 1985.

Kagan, Jerome. *The Nature of the Child.* New York: Basic, 1984.

Kinzie, Mary. "The Man Who Painted Bulls." *Southern Review,* n.s., 16 (1980): 829–52.

Kuhn, Reinhard. *Corruption in Paradise: The Child in Western Literature.* Hanover, N.H.: University Press of New England, 1982.

Leishman, J. B., and Stephen Spender. Introduction to Rilke's *Duino Elegies.* New York: Norton, 1939.

Leppmann, Wolfgang. *Rilke: A Life.* Trans. Wolfgang Leppmann and Russell M. Stockman. New York: Fromm International, 1984.

Lowell, Robert. *Life Studies.* New York: Farrar, 1959.

———. *Notebook.* New York: Farrar, 1970.

———. "Randall Jarrell." In *RJ,* 101–17.

Lowell, Robert, et al., eds. *Randall Jarrell, 1914–1965.* New York: Farrar, 1967.

Mazzaro, Jerome. "Between Two Worlds: The Post-Modernism of Randall Jarrell." In *Crit. Essays,* 82–100.

Meyers, Jeffrey. "The Death of Randall Jarrell." *Virginia Quarterly Review* 58 (1982): 450–67.

———. *Manic Power: Robert Lowell and His Circle.* New York: Arbor House, 1987.

———. "Randall Jarrell: A Bibliography of Criticism." *Bulletin of Bibliography* 39, no. 4 (1982): 227–34.

———. "Randall Jarrell: The Paintings in the Poems." *Southern Review,* n.s., 20 (1984): 300–315.

Miller, Alice. *The Drama of the Gifted Child.* Trans. Ruth Ward. New York: Basic, 1981.

———. *For Your Own Good: Hidden Cruelty in Child-Rearing and the Roots of Violence.* Trans. H. and H. Hannum. New York: Farrar, 1984.

———. *Thou Shalt Not Be Aware: Society's Betrayal of the Child.* Trans. H. and H. Hannum. New York: Meridian, 1986.

Pattison, Robert. *The Child Figure in English Literature.* Athens: University of Georgia Press, 1978.

Piaget, Jean. *The Child's Conception of the World.* Trans. J. and A. Tomlinson. Totowa, N.J.: Littlefield, 1979.

————. *The Language and Thought of the Child.* Trans. Marjorie Gabain. New York: Humanities Press, 1952.

————. *The Moral Judgment of the Child.* Trans. Marjorie Gabain. New York: Free Press, 1965.

Postman, Neil. *The Disappearance of Childhood.* New York: Laurel, 1984.

Pratt, William. "Jarrell as Critic." *Mississippi Quarterly* 54 (1981): 477–84.

Pritchard, William H. "Randall Jarrell: Poet-Critic." In *Crit. Essays,* 120–39.

Quinn, Sister M. Bernetta. "Jarrell's Desert of the Heart." *Analects* 1 (Spring 1961): 24–28.

————. *The Metamorphic Tradition in Modern Poetry.* New Brunswick, N.J.: Rutgers University Press, 1955.

————. *Randall Jarrell.* Boston: Twayne, 1981.

————. "Randall Jarrell: Landscapes of Life and *Life.*" *Shenandoah* 20 (1969): 49–78.

————. "Thematic Imagery in the Poetry of Randall Jarrell." *Southern Review,* n.s., 5 (1969): 126–36.

————. "Warren and Jarrell: The Remembered Child." *Southern Literary Journal* 8 (1976): 24–40.

Ransom, John Crowe. "The Rugged Way of Genius." In *RJ,* 155–81.

————. "Tribute at Yale." *Alumni News,* University of North Carolina at Greensboro (Spring 1966): 8.

Rilke, Rainer Maria. *The Notebooks of Malte Laurids Brigge.* Trans. Stephen Mitchell. New York: Random, 1982.

————. *Selected Poetry of Rainer Maria Rilke.* Trans. Stephen Mitchell. New York: Vintage, 1984.

Rosenthal, M. L. *Randall Jarrell.* Minneapolis: University of Minnesota Press, 1972.

Sale, Roger. *Fairy Tales and After: From Snow White to E. B. White.* Cambridge, Mass.: Harvard University Press, 1978.

Schiller, Friedrich von. *Naive and Sentimental Poetry and On the Sublime.* Trans. Julias A. Elias. New York: Frederick Ungar, 1966.

Schorsch, Anita. *Images of Childhood: An Illustrated Social History.* New York: Main Street Press, 1979.

Schwartz, Delmore. "The Dream from Which No One Wakes." In *Crit. Essays,* 19–20.

Sendak, Maurice. *Caldecott and Co.: Notes on Pictures and Books.* New York: Farrar, 1988.

Shapiro, Karl. "The Death of Randall Jarrell." In *RJ*, 195–229.

Simpson, Eileen. *Poets in Their Youth.* New York: Random, 1982.

Stead, Christina. *The Man Who Loved Children.* Introduction by Randall Jarrell. New York: Holt, 1965.

Stevens, Wallace. *The Collected Poems.* New York: Knopf, 1954.

Taylor, Eleanor Ross. "Greensboro Days." In *RJ*, 233–40.

Taylor, Peter. "Randall Jarrell." In *RJ*, 241–52.

Travisano, Thomas J. *Elizabeth Bishop: Her Artistic Development.* Charlottesville: University Press of Virginia, 1988.

Tyler, Parker. "The Dramatic Lyrism of Randall Jarrell." In *Crit. Essays*, 140–48.

Updike, John. Review of *Fly by Night*, by Randall Jarrell. *New York Times Book Review*, 14 November 1976, 25, 36. Reprinted in *Crit. Essays*, 57–60.

Watson, Robert. "Randall Jarrell: The Last Years." In *RJ*, 257–73.

Williams, Margery. *The Velveteen Rabbit.* Garden City: Doubleday, n.d.

Winn, Marie. *Children Without Childhood.* New York: Penguin, 1984.

Wordsworth, William. *Poetical Works.* London: Oxford, 1969.

Wright, Stuart. *Randall Jarrell: A Descriptive Bibliography, 1929–1983.* Charlottesville: University Press of Virginia, 1985.

Vendler, Helen. *Part of Nature, Part of Us.* Cambridge, Mass.: Harvard University Press, 1980.

Zanderer, Leo. "Randall Jarrell: About and For Children." *The Lion and the Unicorn* 2, no. 1 (Spring 1978): 73–93.

Index